TRUE STORIES OF COURAGE, HUMOR, HOPE & LOVE

SANTA'S GIFT

with reflections by
SIR ELTON JOHN, WARREN BUFFETT
and more

JEFFREY W. COMMENT

All of the author's proceeds
will be donated to the
Elizabeth Glaser Pediatric AIDS Foundation

For general information on our other products and services, or technical support, please contact our Customer Care Department within the United States at 800-762-2974, outside the United States at (317) 572-3993 or fax (317) 572-4002.

Wiley also publishes its books in a variety of electronic formats. Some content that appears in print may not be available in electronic books.

ISBN: 0-471-22515-0

Printed in the United States of America

10 9 8 7 6 5 4 3 2

This book is dedicated to the thousands of kids we have met over the years who have demonstrated such courage in spite of their illnesses and pain. It is their great spirit that inspired Santa, and will in time through this book inspire others to face the world and its adversity with new hope.

CONTENTS

Foreword by
WARREN BUFFETT

Many years ago, Ben Graham, my friend and teacher, told me of a goal he had set for himself. Each day, he would attempt to do something creative, something generous, and something foolish. I think Ben included the third activity to avoid sounding "preachy" in recommending the first two.

Jeff Comment has run Helzberg Diamond Shops for Berkshire Hathaway since the day we acquired it in 1995. He's a superb businessman, and I've yet to see him do anything that could conceivably be characterized as foolish. As CEO of Berkshire, I feel lucky to be associated with him.

But, more important, I also feel proud. Jeff is a great citizen, and he has blended Ben's recommendation for creative and generous acts into a program that has lifted the spirits of thousands of ill or disabled children. When Jeff presents his "I Am Loved"® bear, the child receiving it knows that the message is true: The girl or boy can see it in the eyes of the big fellow standing there in the red suit. That's a gift that has more therapeutic value than any pill or wonder drug can deliver.

As I write this, my grandson, Howard, is in his fifth week in the hospital recovering from injuries suffered in an automobile accident. I have seen first-hand the effect of family love on the healing process. Howie bears his pain far more easily when love and humor are in the room with him. He's getting that in abundance, but not all hospital-bound children are so lucky.

In his Santa activities, Jeff has redefined "family," embracing all children as if they were his own. By doing so, he has converted youngsters with impassive faces and lifeless behavior into the excited and eager human beings they were meant to be. His stories about those children will inspire you, as they have me.

ACKNOWLEDGMENTS

Dodie McCracken—Collaborator

For six years of dedication to the Santa's Gift program and her tireless effort in bringing this book to life. She's the #1 Elf. Dodie McCracken is the founder of the public relations firm, McCracken & Associates, headquartered in Winnetka, IL.

Theresa Foy DiGeronimo—Writer

For being patient with the author and sharing her gift of writing with all our readers. Theresa DiGeronimo is an adjunct professor of English at The William Paterson University of New Jersey and has over 35 nonfiction books currently in publication.

Kate Carr—Friend and Partner

For introducing us to many wonderful people who have already caught the spirit of loving and giving to children. Kate Carr is the president and chief executive officer of the Elizabeth Glaser Pediatric AIDS Foundation.

Kristen and Ryan—Santa's Kids

Kristen, for writing the first idea "Jonathan Through Santa's Eyes," and Ryan, for reminding Dad to chase the right dreams.

Martha—Mrs. Claus

For being my love, my partner, and encourager all these years.

To All Our Hospital Partners

Children's Mercy Hospital—Kansas City, MO

University of Chicago Children's Hospital—Chicago, IL

Cook County Children's Hospital—Chicago, IL

Children's Memorial Medical Center—Chicago, IL

Rush-Presbyterian-St. Luke's Medical Center—Chicago, IL

Advocate Lutheran General Children's Hospital—Chicago, IL

Children's Medical Center—Dallas, TX

Children's Hospital of Philadelphia—Philadelphia, PA

St. Christopher's Hospital for Children—Philadelphia, PA

Children's National Medical Center—Washington, DC

Children's Hospitals & Clinics—Minneapolis, MN

The Children's Medical Center—Dayton, OH

INTRODUCTION

When I was in my early 20s, I had no idea what the word *philanthropic* meant. I donated to charity and I pitched in when our community collected food for the poor, but I had no real concept of what it meant to truly give of myself to help someone else. Then one day I was walking down a street in Miami when I saw a long line of men and women outside a storefront waiting to get into a soup kitchen. At first, the scene made me feel uncomfortable because many of these people smelled bad and they wore old and torn clothing. As I began to hurry by, I glanced inside and saw businesspeople just like myself working together to prepare the meals for the hungry who waited by the door. That intrigued me. I went in and found myself hooked. For the next four years, I spent every Friday afternoon serving food to the poor and hungry. The people at the company I worked for kidded me about this. However, within the next year, that soup kitchen was completely staffed on Fridays by about 20 of my colleagues. That was the first time I saw for myself that the good feeling you get from giving to others could be contagious!

Many years later, in 1995, Helzberg Diamonds hosted a Christmas party for a local Kansas City charity. As the company CEO, it was my job to be Santa Claus that year and greet the disadvantaged children who came to enjoy some Christmas treats and meet old St. Nick. Underneath the red velvet costume, I was just a retailer, but I quickly realized that to these kids who were carrying the burden of premature adulthood, Santa Claus represented hope. Throughout the day, these kids asked Santa to reunite parents, bring home a sibling, or make a mother or father stop drinking. This was the day I realized that Santa is much more than a mythical character who slides down chimneys; I knew in my heart that he was the bearer of love, compassion, and new possibilities.

It was that experience that sparked the idea for the "Santa's Gift" project. With another holiday season approaching, I decided to extend Santa's reach beyond our own holiday party to children who were spending their holiday in the hospital—children suffering from illnesses and injuries who needed some cheer and a reason to laugh.

With the help of Helzberg's marketing associates, an ambitious plan for December 1996 began to take shape: Eight major hospitals in five U.S. cities were put on our Christmas list. I wanted to visit every one of the 2,000 children in these hospitals—not just the ones who were well enough to make it to the hospital's party room where Santa could sit as children clamored up onto his knee. (This was the custom during all previous Santa visits.) This Santa also wanted to visit the children who were bedridden, the ones in intensive care, those in the burn units, those undergoing chemotherapy in the oncology units, and even the infants who were too small and too frail to be moved.

I was ready to trade in my suit and tie for a Santa costume. Having been Santa at our own company parties, I realized the freedom it gave me to be even more generous. With Santa a universal symbol of hope and joy that children seem to be able to grasp and hold onto, I was eager to begin my journey in my white beard and red hat to visit kids in pediatric units who would not otherwise have much of a Christmas.

This might not be as easy as I had imagined. What if I looked foolish and embarrassed the company? What if children cried when they saw me? What if I didn't know what to say to make them feel better? I reminded myself that this wasn't about me. I wasn't here to impress others. My fears slowed my steps but I kept moving forward, focusing on my heartfelt intention. I was here because I wanted to give something back and I was sure that working with sick or injured children was where I could do the most good.

Just seconds after arriving at the first hospital, all my concerns about being inadequate or silly were dismissed as the children squealed with joy when I entered their rooms. It was easy to see that I was not there to be judged or evaluated; I was there simply to give and receive unconditional love. I knew immediately that I was in the right place and that it was important for me to do this.

I have returned to these hospitals for seven years now and have met over 15,000 children. Each one of these little tykes had something to teach me. Although it's true that I have witnessed terrible pain and sadness, I have also learned much about the healing power of love, the eternal quality of hope, the comfort of humor, and the depth of human courage. My life has been immensely enriched by these lessons. There is absolutely no doubt that I have received far more than I have given.

In this book, I have gathered stories of some of the many children who have touched my heart. Each one represents hundreds of others who are also struggling with the pain and uncertainty of illness and injury, yet who opened their hearts to welcome me, and who taught me valuable lessons for which I will be forever grateful.

It is my hope that through these stories you may experience that contagious quality of philanthropy. These children may move you to share a little of yourself with someone in need and receive in return the greatest gift of all—a full and rewarding life that has been touched by the heart of another.

Reflection by

SIR ELTON JOHN

Elton John is one of the most successful entertainers of the past 30 years. From his first Top 10 single in the United States—"Your Song"—he has had numerous hits and has also appeared on stage and in films. In the mid-1980s, Elton John became interested in AIDS research, met Ryan White, and formed the Elton John AIDS Foundation. He has donated royalties from his singles to AIDS charities.

I used to think that giving money was what generosity and philanthropy was all about. That was until I spent a week with Ryan White who, at 13, was one of the first and most courageous AIDS activists.

I was with Ryan in Indianapolis in 1990 during the last week of his life. I went to the hospital every day and saw in Ryan and his family humility, generosity, and the ability to forgive during the most tragic and sad circumstances. That week, when, instead of money I gave my time and understood how much it was appreciated, meant so much to me.

That week had a huge impact on me. It was at a time of my life when I was very self-absorbed. I was not behaving very well. I was into drugs and simply out of whack. Ryan's example was the catalyst for me to change my life and get sober and clean and start doing philanthropic work myself.

Many people can't afford to be philanthropic with money, but we all have time we can donate. That is the most important lesson I've learned since Ryan's death. The time I spend with my AIDS Foundation or just talking to people has the most value. There are so many people who need our help. It is important to get involved. When I see how grateful people are, that's the biggest thrill for me. Go see for yourself. The rewards are incredible.

PART I

Stories of
COURAGE

The Story of Jonathan
My Heroes
Parent and Child
The Beauty of Lindsay

Reflection by Kate Carr

THE STORY OF JONATHAN

*O*ur Santa tour had been in progress for just two days when we visited Advocate Lutheran General Children's Hospital in Chicago. It was here during a visit to a little boy named Jonathan, right at the start, that the importance and value of my efforts became crystal clear to me.

As we rode up in the elevator, the nurse informed me that working with these kids was a very tough assignment, even for a seasoned veteran. I wondered what she meant by "these kids." What was I getting myself into? Was something about to happen that I wouldn't be able to handle?

Before I could worry myself into backing out, the elevator doors opened at the fourth floor and we stepped out into the glare of bright hospital lights. It was immediately obvious that there was no holiday cheer ringing in these halls. The medicinal smell of disinfectant and the blur of nurses, doctors, and interns rushing to their patients made me

stop and consider that maybe the jolly ho-ho-hos of Santa would be more disruptive than helpful. This was a no-nonsense, serious place where medical professionals were trying to keep kids alive. I wondered if I was jumping into water over my head.

As I stepped from the elevator, a young intern approached me with a smile that did not belie the urgency in his voice.

"Please come with me," he said very gravely. "There's a young man named Jonathan who's been waiting for you." In a conspiratorial whisper, he added, "I think he's staying alive just until he sees Santa Claus."

Jonathan's room was our first stop on the floor. As we approached the child's room, the intern told me that Jonathan was "on stage" — hospital jargon meaning "about to die." With no time to react to this revelation, I entered the room.

I saw an eleven-year-old boy who looked more like seven or eight. He was so thin his small facial bones pushed out against his pale, sallow skin. His blue eyes sat too large in his shrunken face. Nevertheless, he was alert, sitting in a wheelchair with his straight, blonde hair freshly combed, waiting for Santa. This, I would later learn, was only a wisp of the boy he had been a few years earlier.

Jonathan had been a lovable, huggable, kissable practical joker. He played baseball, soccer, basketball, and football. He liked to tackle and be

ARTWORK BY CHELSEA

We were privileged to have Jonathan in our lives. He was a happy, positive child who befriended everyone he met. His delightful smile and unconditional love, in spite of his illness, was an inspiration to everyone he met. You could not help wanting to smile when you passed him. Even his short visit with "Santa" has affected thousands of hospitalized children every year, as Jeff continues his mission of spreading hope and love every holiday season. The thousands of dollars that have been donated to pediatric AIDS research as a result of Jeff's visit with Jonathan will benefit people all over the world for many years to come. As the years go by, Jon's love continues to flourish as more and more people become involved in spreading his message of love.

MARGE AND BILL STEVENSON, JONATHAN'S PARENTS

tackled. In baseball, he had a good eye and could hit the ball a great distance. He could do everything as well as other boys his age and, in some instances, better!

Jonathan was playing soccer when his parents noticed that just running a short distance would tire him. At first, they thought he was just exhausted from the grind of adjusting to kindergarten but, as the fatigue became more frequent, they took him to their pediatrician. After several tests, Jonathan was diagnosed as HIV-positive. Over the years, he slowly lost his physical functions, including his speech.

Amazingly, he never lost his love of life, his love of a good joke, or his wonderful smile.

When I appeared, Jonathan didn't move, but everyone in the room saw his eyes instantly brighten with excitement. His mother bent down and whispered softly to her son, "Jonathan, Santa has come especially to see you."

"Oh God," I silently prayed. "Give me the courage to do the right thing." I couldn't bear to disappoint this child who looked to me for a small reprieve from his pain and from his thoughts of death.

Volunteerism and giving should be an integral component of any children's hospital. Professionals and others who care for children are automatically "givers"—whether they are nurses, doctors, therapists, or other ancillary staff, they give of themselves in every interaction with a sick child—the obvious "giving" is the application of specific professional/technical skills to help recovery, but there is the other "giving," the emotional support provided to pediatric patients and their parents, the reassurances, the hope (even when situations seem grim), the availability at all hours, the "special touch" that conveys genuine caring. This is but one aspect that distinguishes pediatric health care providers from others.
HENRY MANGURTEN, M.D., CHAIRMAN, DEPARTMENT OF PEDIATRICS,
ADVOCATE LUTHERAN GENERAL CHILDREN'S HOSPITAL

As I pulled up a stool and sat down next to him, an instinct moved me to reach out and cup his hand in my own and give a gentle squeeze. Jonathan was too weak to squeeze back, and his vocal cords were too deteriorated for speech, but he managed a big, gaping smile that spread across his small face. I couldn't have asked for more.

Jonathan's mother told me he'd been practicing a puppet show and then she helped him put a green felt dragon on his hand. Slowly, and with great effort, Jonathan managed to wiggle his fingers as his dragon came to life. I gave a great belly laugh and applauded heartily as Jonathan beamed. Then as I stood to leave, I saw Jonathan's eyes well up with tears that spilled over onto his pallid cheeks. His watery eyes held mine and I couldn't move. Finally, it was Jonathan who released me. He softly patted the back of my hand as if to say, "It's okay, Santa; you can go now." He then waved his green dragon at me to say goodbye.

As I turned around to leave, I found there was no one else in the room. Where was my entourage that had consisted of a public relations person, a hospital events coordinator, and a nurse? I learned later that they had each left the room to hide their own tears. How heartbreaking it is to watch a child who is losing his fight for life look so courageous. It occurred to me that it was sad and ironic that all of these people could leave the room to regain their composure, but Jonathan could not. The one person who had the most reason to run and hide from his emotional pain could not escape his own tragic reality. Yet, even as the tears dripped off his cheeks, he never lost his smile. It was a powerful moment for me in which I suddenly grasped the incredible depth of character children have. This child, who would probably never see his next birthday, showed me what true courage looks like. I saw that it exists in its purest form only when it stands alone without anger, bitterness, or self-pity.

I also saw that courage grows stronger when it is shared with others. As my own tears welled to the brink, I borrowed from the courage of this young boy and determined that I wouldn't take my sadness into another child's room. There were others on the ward who needed to see Santa, and I needed to bring them all the joy and happiness I could muster. In his small, precious way, Jonathan made me understand that by dressing up as Santa and waddling through countless corridors with my jingling bells, shouting "Merry Christmas," I was doing the right thing. If this meant something to only one child, as it had to Jonathan, then it would be worth all the time and all the visits to the 2,000 kids

I would encounter on this incredible and touching journey. Jonathan gave me courage.

From Jonathan, we can all gain the valuable legacy of courage. When you need to be brave to do what's right, when you need courage to stand up for your beliefs, and when you feel weak and frightened—think of Jonathan. He will remind you that it's in the tough times that you need to keep the smile and find the resources deep inside that will help you endure. He will remind you that it is when you are down that you have your greatest opportunity to help others in a lasting way. Thoughts of Jonathan will remind you that real courage is contagious and that it can give those around you the strength they may need in times of tribulation. Whenever you're tempted to give up, to quit, or to let anger, bitterness, or self-pity win, think of Jonathan.

Jonathan died of AIDS on January 22, 1997. That was the night that I pledged I would write the book you are now holding. It is my hope that when you see just how much you gain by giving that you will be moved to share your time with others in need.

MY HEROES

*n*othing prepared me for what I saw the first time I entered the pediatric burn unit at Cook County Children's Hospital in Chicago. I'll never forget the distinct odor of singed flesh and medicated ointments that permeated the air as I walked through the heavy double doors. The children, whose burns varied in severity, were wrapped up in white gauze. One child might have an entire arm wrapped; another the whole upper body, while some are completely wrapped with only their eyes, nose, and mouth visible. Some, especially those in the intensive care burn unit, are unconscious, having been sedated by heavy doses of pain medication. Whether sedated or not, most of the children are in torment; it is heartbreaking to hear their soft moans and whimpers. Unlike the children I had visited in other units, I knew that many of these youngsters would wear the scars of their pain for the rest of their lives.

For this reason, the hospital has a staff of dedicated child-life workers. These professionals use play, recreation, education, self-expression,

and theories of child development to minimize psychological trauma for both the child and his or her family. The child-life worker who accompanied me on my first tour of this unit was an experienced professional who had worked with burned children for over 15 years. She referred to her work as her calling, rather than her job—a remark I didn't fully understand until I had spent more time with these children and their families. It didn't take me long to realize that no one can care for these suffering little ones day after day without a sense of dedication and purpose that goes far beyond a paycheck. As she escorted me down the hall, she told me she would understand if I needed a break or if I wanted to cut the visit short. She was well aware that this job was not for everyone. I was beginning to doubt that I was brave enough to spend 15 minutes here, never mind 15 years!

But shortly after I entered (more quietly than usual without ringing bells or loud ho-ho-hos) and saw the parents turn to give me half-hearted smiles, I knew Santa had work to do. Written on their faces was an unspoken anguish as they sat helplessly beside their children, unable to do anything—not even touch them, in some cases.

I sat down next to one mother whose son's head, face, and shoulders were heavily bandaged; I held her hand and said, "Santa loves you, you know." She took a deep breath, sort of smiled, and after a moment's silence asked if I'd like to see a picture of her son. She handed me one of those wallet-sized school portraits so familiar to all parents. As tears welled in her eyes, she said, "Before the fire, he was so handsome. Look, see that dimple right there?" she asked pausing to control her shaky voice. "He got that from me."

I looked carefully at the picture and saw a beautiful little boy who looked to be about nine years old. His toothy smile lit up a freckled face and sure enough, a deep dimple marked his right cheek. Judging by the extent of the boy's bandages, I could guess that his face and upper body had been severely burned and would certainly be scarred. What could I possibly say to this heartbroken mother?

Cook County Children's Hospital is a public hospital that provides excellent medical care to all children regardless of ability to pay. Funds are not generally available for the "extras," that is, children's gifts, hospital parties, special needs, and other amenities. Without people like Jeff, who give generously of their time, affection, and resources (also known as "love"), our patients would not get these much-needed gifts. Volunteers fill these difficult moments and times by giving that special something that each child deserves.

PAM BOORAS, COOK COUNTY CHILDREN'S HOSPITAL

"Memories of the past, like this picture, are gifts," I began. "But there's also hope for the future. With the help of these wonderful doctors and nurses, your son will regain his health and grow to become whatever he wants to be."

Weary from strain and sleepless nights she looked at me and said, "Santa, that's the only hope I have, and it sustains me every day."

After a parting hug, I stood to move on to the next child. Turning back to wave goodbye, this tired mom gave me a wonderful smile, and sure enough — there was that big dimple in her right cheek.

As I moved through the unit, I continued to find it very difficult to look at children in this condition. Not solely because of their extensive bandages, disfigurements, and obvious pain, but because it broke my heart to see them suffering so. In a perfect world, all children would be healthy and happy; they would be outside running around and laughing. However, it becomes clear to anyone who steps into a pediatric burn unit that this is not a perfect world.

It is not perfect in many ways. I learned from one of the doctors on this floor that my royal greeting from some of the kids is because a disproportionate number of the children who are admitted to the hospital for burns come from dysfunctional homes. These homes don't have smoke detectors; there are no protective parents to watch the pot of boiling water on the stove, and sometimes fire or boiling water is used to discipline kids. When that's the case, Santa represents a safe haven and a promise of love. His magic takes them away from the physical and emotional pain of their own reality into a fantasy world where they can enjoy the simple pleasure of just being kids.

One of these huggable little ones was a six-year-old who was starting on the road to recovery. He had been scalded badly by hot grease that splattered on his face and upper body. The bandages had been removed and the raw scars were now exposed. Despite the disfigurement, it was easy to see that this child had a beautiful spirit. He sat up and clapped his hands as I poked my head into the room. Though he winced in pain at the movement, his face lit up with joy. The nurse told me that she hadn't seen him move that much or that quickly since he arrived!

"Santa!" he yelled and then clasped his hands over his mouth as he remembered that his roommate was sleeping. In an excited whisper, he continued, "I'm so glad you found me! Ya know what I really want for Christmas?"

Of course, I had no idea, so I asked, "What would you like from Santa?"

"I want my mommy to come visit me," he said with great hope. "Can you bring her here?"

"Well," I said stalling for time so I could think of a good answer, "I'll talk to the doctors about that, but while you're getting better, I want you to do what the doctors and nurses tell you so you can go home as soon as you're ready. And remember, no matter where you are on Christmas Eve, Santa will come by and check on you while you're sleeping because he loves you."

"Okay," he replied slowly. "Thank you."

This was one of the thousands of children who try to accept what life has handed them—even when it hurts and they don't understand why. How, I wondered, could these children get up in the morning and struggle through another day of pain, uncertainty, and heartache? After giving the question much thought, the answer, it seems to me, is that they have found deep inside their souls the supply of courage reserved for times of crisis. Humans throughout history have proven that true courage is found when we push past our limits of endurance, when we handle more than we thought we could, when we face the impossible and imagine what still might be.

The children, the caring parents, and medical professionals in the burn units around the world are my heroes. They are defying almost impossible odds, yet they persevere. Fire may be able to destroy homes and possessions and it can disfigure bodies, but these people have shown me that there is one place it cannot reach—the heart.

When you look for examples of courage to inspire and motivate you, look no further than those all around you who are struggling with life's dark moments and who keep getting up in the morning anyway. In addition, look to those who stand beside them giving support and encouragement, those who put aside their own fears to give strength to others.

Then ask yourself if you'd like to be someone's hero. It's not so very hard to do if you have the willingness to share your own supply of courage and strength with someone who is faltering under the weight of tragedy and suffering. These people are all around us, reaching out for help. They are in our soup kitchens; they are in our senior centers; they are in our prisons and hospitals. They are in our neighborhoods and our churches. Why not find the courage today to become someone's hero?

If I sit back and just read about the problems of the world, I feel victimized. But if I do something and become part of the solution, the problems of the world do not hurt quite so much.

TED DANSON, ACTOR

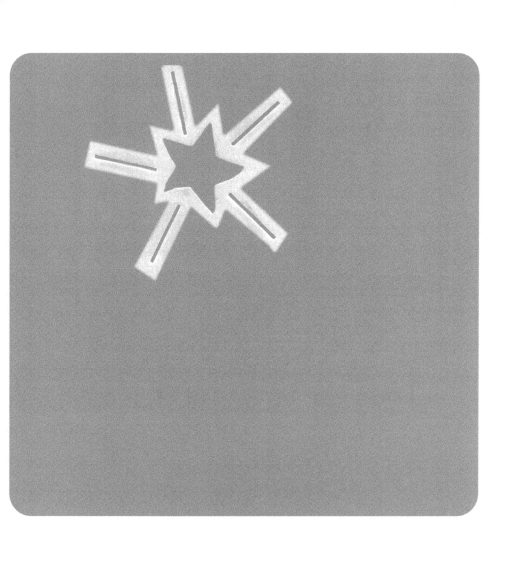

PARENT AND CHILD

*I*n hospital after hospital and in city after city, I am always impressed by the supportive and upbeat attitude I see in the parents of the children I visit. Even though all my visits take place during the work day, I frequently see parents who put everything else in their lives aside to be by their children when they need them. Some keep vigils round the clock, sleeping in the oversized chairs placed next to the children's beds; some entertain frightened little ones for hours with stories, puppet shows, and board games; some gather with mom, dad, grandma, and grandpa all together, while others take turns at the bedside one at a time. Whatever the situation, I am continually amazed by the emotional strength and optimism that I see.

One day during a visit to Children's Mercy Hospital in Kansas City, Missouri, I saw a mom sitting in a hallway all by herself and learned the truth about all parents of hospitalized children: The cheerful faces and happy outlooks are facades they wear for the sake of their children. This woman just an hour earlier had been laughing with Santa and tickling her daughter; now she sat lifelessly in a chair outside her daughter's room, vacantly staring at the wall and gripping a cup of tepid coffee. Her face was drawn from strain and fatigue and there was great pain in her body posture. I was deeply moved by her struggle and stood by in silent admiration. This broken parent would, in a few more minutes, take a deep breath, stand up, smile, and go back into her child's hospital room, masking her own anguish to appear strong for her child. At that moment I understood, perhaps for the first time, what it really means to be courageous.

Working with HIV-infected mothers is a blessing for me. I found out that I was infected with HIV in December 1996. The most painful moment of my life was when my child Nomthunzi died because he also was infected. My work involves counseling pregnant mothers about their HIV status. I have seen many mothers become stronger from hearing my personal story. It also helps me to know that I am making a difference. I am often asked why I am always happy and smiling to everybody who walks in the door. I smile because there is hope, but I'm still hurting inside. I still cry when I think of the many young lives that are wasted each day.

FLORENCE NGOBENI, BARAGWANATH HOSPITAL,

SOWETO, SOUTH AFRICA

Later in the day I was reminded again how very difficult it is to be strong, brave, and welcoming when it is your child who is seriously injured. I was making my Santa stops on the surgical floor and with a few loud ho-ho-hos began to enter the room of a young girl who'd just had surgery after a serious car accident. I was abruptly stopped at

> *Everyone dies. The choice and the challenge are in how we choose to live. And the more meaning you find in your life, the more reason you have to live.*
>
> ELIZABETH GLASER, COFOUNDER,
THE ELIZABETH GLASER PEDIATRIC AIDS FOUNDATION

the door by a woman who announced to me sternly that her daughter would tolerate no visitors. Although I worried that there might be a child in there who really needed a reason to smile, I honored her mother's judgment and moved back out into the hall.

Here I encountered a child about eight years old with a beautiful head of curly black hair who boldly rolled his wheelchair up to me and tugged at my sleeve. "Hey Santa! Hey Santa!" he yelled. "I want to tell you what I want for Christmas!" I knelt beside him and listened intently as he rattled off a rather extensive Christmas list. "Okay, okay!" I laughed. "I'll try to remember all of that if you're a very good boy and do what the doctors and nurses and your mom and dad tell you to do." Then I stood up and enjoyed his shrieks of delight when I placed a teddy bear in his lap. As his laughter mingled with the sound of my bells, I wondered if the mother who'd turned me away was bothered by the commotion. However, more children were waiting and I put the worry aside and moved on.

I had just finished my rounds that day and, tired, I headed back toward the elevator when I heard someone far down the hall shout, "Santa! Wait!" It was the mother who had refused me entrance to her child's room. "I'm sorry I sent you away before," she said, her eyes filling with tears. "Please come see my daughter. I think maybe she really needs you." The North Pole, I decided, could wait as I delayed my departure with renewed energy.

The car accident had left this seven-year-old child severely disfigured. She had undergone massive facial reconstructive surgery and would have to endure many more operations to remove the physical scars she suffered. Sitting beside her bed, it was difficult to

A quote posted on the wall in the Volunteer Services office at Children's Mercy Hospital is: "How wonderful that no one need wait a single moment to improve the world." This quote is from Anne Frank. Whether a volunteer is reading to a child, assisting families at an information desk, or organizing children's clothing in the Kid's Closet, the love they share is reflected on the faces of our children. Our volunteers give much more than their time and extensive talents. They give the gift of caring. They give because a smile on the face of a child is a priceless gift. They give because they see no need to "wait a single moment to improve the world."

CHILD LIFE DEPARTMENT, CHILDREN'S MERCY HOSPITAL

come up with meaningful words to soothe her, but, as I've discovered, words are not always the most important things. As I held her hand, I thought I saw a smile peek through her mask of bandages and I knew the magic of Santa had once again touched the heart of a child in pain. As I looked over at the girl's mother, I saw that she too saw her daughter's smile. With her

jaw clenched in an attempt to hold back the tears that were now slipping down her cheeks, she nodded her thanks. I thought how very brave she will have to be to see her daughter through this difficult time. She will be called on to make a thousand decisions that, though they will tear at her heart, they will be in the best interest of her child. Allowing me into the room was just one small step in a very long journey.

Having raised two children, I've always known that it takes courage to be a parent: Courage to set a good example in words and deeds, courage to say no when yes would be so much easier, courage to stand back and let a child learn a life lesson without running interference throughout each day and year of their growth. However, I had no idea of the depth of that well until I watched the parents of sick and injured children. At first, in the bustle of the hospital environment, all attention is on the child. It is emotionally draining and at the same time uplifting to see the courage these children display in the face of pain, illness, and uncertainty. But then I noticed that in family after family, like the support beams of a home that are hidden and taken for granted, it was the parents who stood tall in the background and kept it all together. Without any formal instruction or direction, they each found the courage to give their children the gift of emotional strength despite their own heartbreak. Day after day they put aside their own fatigue and worry and offered a smile, words of encouragement, and moments of distraction.

These parents have taught me so much about what it means to be a strong and courageous person. I now know it does not mean being fearless; it means being afraid and smiling anyway as you carefully move forward one step at a time. I pray that God will help all of us to be more like these parents when we are tempted to put our own feelings and needs before those who are smaller, weaker, and more needy.

THE BEAUTY OF LINDSAY

One of the things I appreciate more as I grow older is the beauty of children. There's something about children—no matter whether they are short or tall, a little skinny or a little overweight, and yes, even those who are injured or fighting some sort of dreadful disease—that is absolutely beautiful. It truly is one of the greatest gifts that I get every year as I visit hospitals—the smiles, the laughter, and even the words of simple wisdom that come from kids give them a beauty that's hard to describe.

I've seen this same kind of beauty in some adults—but it's rare. I think this special quality is more often found in children because it's rooted in the way that they view the world—with honesty and hope. Even though many of them have faced physical difficulties and know plenty about the trials and tribulations of life, they still believe in the goodness of human nature. The selfishness and greed that corrupts our society have not yet disillusioned them. Most have not been victims of intentional cruelty or unforgivable betrayal. You can see an innocence in their eyes that gives them great hope, great dreams, and the desire to be physically whole again so they might one day enjoy their as yet unfulfilled potential.

So often Santa sees this in children—whether in the burn unit where they're bound in salve and bandages, or in the oncology unit where they're attached to IVs delivering their chemotherapy, or on the orthopedic floor where they're struggling with broken bones and unwieldy casts. All of them bravely face each new day, holding on to the unspoken promise of the fullness of life. How many of us can say the same?

I particularly remember feeling this positive energy from one eighteen-year-old young lady named Lindsay whom I met two years in a row on my Santa rounds at the University of Chicago Children's Hospital. I first met Lindsay in December 2000 when I stopped in the oncology unit where I visited with many children bravely facing the difficult therapies involving chemotherapy, radiation, and other treatments. Each was fighting a battle to rid his or her body of some terrible cancer. Before we entered Lindsay's room, the nurse told me that four years ago Lindsay was diagnosed with osteogenic sarcoma. In her fight to beat this form of bone cancer, she had received a stem cell transplant a few weeks earlier and was now visiting the hospital as an outpatient several days each week for blood transfusions to boost her bone marrow. How different her life is, I thought, from other healthy eighteen-year-olds.

Life, love, and happiness . . . is to help another human, to make a child smile, to go through life's journeys with courage, humor, and grace.

ROBERT KEMPLER,
SAMUEL AARON INTERNATIONAL

When I entered the room, Lindsay was sitting up in her bed sporting a colorful bandana on her head, masking her baldness. However, it wasn't the bandana or even the mischievous wink from her mom who sat next to her that caught Santa's eye, it was the smile on her beautiful face. It was that funny kind of grin that a teen gives when she wants to smile but isn't quite sure if a full smile would be respectably cool.

I introduced myself and waited to see if she would play along. I felt grateful and relieved when Lindsay welcomed Santa to sit on the side of her bed. After only a few short moments of conversation, I knew this young lady was very special and the memory of her would stay with me forever. Here she was fighting off death and yet her thoughts were on the work of Santa and the magic of hope that he brings to little kids. She wasn't willing to spend one moment dwelling on her illness or talking about it—she was excited that Santa was going to make lots of little kids happy that day. Although Santa had entered the room hoping to give encouragement to a young lady facing a difficult future, I have to admit that I took away more encouragement for myself than I gave to her. There was that beauty I often talk about— that optimistic courage that won't be tarnished by the weariness and disappointment that undermines so many of my own good intentions.

The children that Santa visits during December never realize that they give him an incredible gift that lasts for the next 12 months until he returns. That's the gift of their joy, their stamina, and their courage. Often when I would reflect on the visits of the year 2000, I would come back to a dozen or so young people who had especially impressed me; Lindsay was one of those.

In December 2001, Santa was once again visiting the University of Chicago Children's Hospital when, just before entering a room, the nurse said to me, "Santa, last year you had a wonderful visit with this young lady. You might not remember her, but her name is Lindsay." I paused at the door's entrance and said, "I remember her well."

As I entered the room, I felt a sense of joy as if I was revisiting an old friend. The image of her face had been with me for the past 12 months and I was looking forward to seeing her again. The joy, however, was tempered with sadness at the thought that she was once again in the hospital—which couldn't be good news. I had to gather courage on my own part so that the old positive Santa gusto would be there. I should have known that would not be necessary with Lindsay. As I entered her room, the first thing I saw was that silly, wonderful grin. She patted the side of her bed, inviting me once again to sit. No tears, no sad stories, no anger. Lindsay was still bravely fighting for her life with dignity and courage.

After a big hug, I told Lindsay that my visit with her the year before was a memorable experience and, although I was sad to see that she still needed treatment, I was glad she was scheduled for it on that particular day so that we had a chance to chat again. I was excited to tell Lindsay that I had been offered the opportunity to gather some of the stories of the children I met as Santa and put them in a book. "It would be my great pleasure," I said, "if you would share with me your thoughts so that I can share them with my readers."

Lindsay was thrilled to help and we made plans to talk at length at a later time. Right now there were several hundred children waiting and Santa had to move on. But, I promised, we would talk again soon.

Sadly, I was not able to keep that promise.

When the Santa tour of 2001 ended, I made phone contact with Lindsay's mother to arrange an interview with her spunky daughter. However, before the scheduled date, Lindsay died. Through the heartbreak of this news, I am comforted by the gifts she gave me. Because of Lindsay, I now have the courage to do things in my life that I didn't think I could do before; she inspired me to keep going and believing even when reality suggests the effort might be futile. This gift will stay with me throughout my life because I won't let my few moments with Lindsay ever grow weak in memory.

Dedicated to Lindsay Green— September 5, 1982–January 13, 2002.

ARTWORK BY ARTHUR

Reflection by

KATE CARR

Kate Carr is the president and chief executive officer of the Elizabeth Glaser Pediatric AIDS Foundation. Elizabeth Glaser, Susan DeLaurentis, and Susie Zeegen cofounded this organization in 1988. These three friends were compelled to take action after Elizabeth discovered that she, her daughter Ariel, and son Jake were all HIV-infected due to a tainted blood transfusion delivered after the birth of Ariel. Through this tragedy, Elizabeth, Susan, and Susie learned of the need for education and compassion, but also found that research money was desperately needed. The mission was clear—to get money into the hands of researchers as quickly as possible to find answers for children infected with HIV. Sadly, Elizabeth Glaser died in 1994 but her vision, passion, and mission live on in the Foundation and its work. On December 1, 1997—World AIDS Day—the Foundation officially changed its name to the Elizabeth Glaser Pediatric AIDS Foundation as a tribute to Elizabeth's legacy and inspiration in working to find the answers that will lead to better treatments and prevention of HIV infection in infants and children, to reduce and prevent HIV transmission from mother to child, and to accelerate the discovery of new treatments for other serious and life-threatening pediatric diseases.

To be courageous requires no exceptional qualifications, no magic formula, and no special combination of time, place, and circumstances. It's an opportunity that eventually is presented to us all. In the words of John F. Kennedy from *Profiles in Courage*, "Courage is defined as the state or quality of mind or spirit that enables us to face danger with self-possession, confidence, and resolution."

As a mother of three, I have found the most rewarding work in my life because I was inspired by the courage of another mother. Elizabeth Glaser took a tragic circumstance and turned it into an opportunity to change the world. She saw that children were ignored in an epidemic that was sweeping the world, and she decided to take action. From a UCLA commencement address she gave in 1993, I found a lesson on this point. She told the students that in her circumstance she could easily point the finger of blame. She could point it at the government, the medical research institutions, the health insurance companies, or even at God. "But," she said, "pointing fingers does not make anything better. You must do something.

Each of you can look at the country, the world, and see where we are failing—don't just complain about it. Change it. Do something about it."

When you and I look at the world and see a sick child, a homeless man, a starving family, such problems can appear to be overwhelming—too large for one person to make a difference. However, Elizabeth Glaser demonstrated through her leadership that we can all make a difference. "The hardest

Giving money to help fight HIV and AIDS in children makes my heart feel really good. I get really excited knowing that I have raised more money to help fight the disease. When I give up buying myself something pretty or something I like, and then I send my money to the Elizabeth Glaser Pediatrics AIDS Foundation every month, I remember that there are lots of kids like me out there that won't get a chance to enjoy pretty things either if we don't find a cure. When I give like I do, it also shows other people it is important to help others, too. It would make the world a much better place to live in if we try to help one another. It is really important. We all need to share what we have.

NATASHA ANN HEES, AGE 8,
KAMLOOPS, BRITISH COLUMBIA, CANADA

step," she said, "was the first one, and after that we just kept putting one foot in front of the other, knowing that with each step we have contributed something."

Finding the courage to take that first step isn't always easy. Courage and fear are tightly intertwined. When I am afraid, my natural instinct is to pull away, to avoid that which is frightening. In life, we encounter many things that we think we simply can't face, but courage is recognizing that fear and moving forward. Elizabeth was afraid to disclose the tragedy in her family at a time when people with HIV/AIDS were feared, ostracized, and driven out of their communities. Nevertheless, she stepped forward and became a forceful advocate on behalf of children who didn't have the ability to articulate their needs. She decided to act rather than hide. Being afraid and acting with resolution takes true courage.

The stories in this book are about children and families who are facing their worst fears and still showing their courage. We are both touched and inspired by their actions. Without this kind of action in the face of fear, it is impossible to move forward. That is the spirit that drives the Foundation Elizabeth created: We have to believe that what we do today, despite the difficulties we face, can make things better tomorrow. This belief is driven by a deeply held value that the well being of another is bigger than self-interest. From this, we find our compassion and understanding and ultimately our personal reward.

In her book *In the Absence of Angels,* Elizabeth Glaser tells us all: "Ari's life had meaning and there were lessons to be learned from it. She was a courageous little girl who gallantly accepted her life and lived it as thoroughly as she could. She never cried about not being able to go to school or being unable to see a friend. She never felt sorry for herself, nor did she ever give in or give up. Ariel had wisdom, strength, and courage. In my weaker moments, I try to be at least as strong as she was. Her life presents a challenge to all of us to do at least as well as Ari did. Everyone dies . . . the choice and the challenge are in how we choose to live. The more meaning you find in your life, the more reason you have to live."

In my work, I see children and families who courageously face the diagnosis of a serious or life-ending disease. I also see parents who must find the courage to go on after the death of a child. They wake up each morning and take one more step through this difficult time in their lives. Although it is painful to watch, their courage is inspirational, teaching us to keep moving forward in tough times, to keep reaching out. It is a reminder that being courageous isn't found only in highly visible heroic actions. Courage can be found in our everyday, ordinary lives when we take the opportunity to step outside ourselves to help another person. It can be something as simple as taking the time to hold someone's hand and say, "I understand, and I will help." A simple act of kindness in the face of adversity is sometimes difficult to summon, but the rewards are readily apparent in the radiant faces of those touched.

PART II

Stories of
HUMOR

Bald Is Beautiful
Poker Faces
One Last Stop
No Two Kids Are Alike

Reflection by Norman Lear

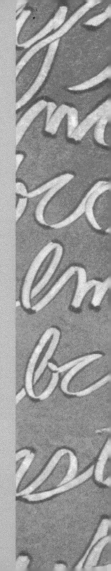

Bald Is Beautiful

I find it difficult to visit pediatric cancer wards. The children here are having surgery, blood transfusions, or undergoing chemotherapy and suffering terribly from the side effects. Many have lost their hair and look malnourished due to excessive weight loss. Here, there is much more frightened silence than laughter. Here, children who should not have to think about how long they will live often count each day as a victory. As difficult as it is for me—the businessman—to watch these children struggle, Santa is right at home. Here, Santa has the magical job of making kids forget, for just a very short time, that they are any different from any other kid.

On a tour of the pediatric oncology floor at the University of Chicago Children's Hospital, a nurse escorted me from room to room up and down the hallways. We always knocked and asked permission to enter because sometimes these children can be too sick or too upset even for Santa. However, on this day, everyone was up for some fun—

everyone except Chuck who refused me admittance. He took one look at me and said with absolutely no emotion, "I stopped believing in Santa a long time ago."

Chuck was a twenty-year-old who had probably had trouble believing in a lot of things since he was diagnosed the summer before with osteogenic sarcoma in his shoulder joint. This is a bone cancer that strikes children whose bones are still growing—even children like Chuck who are six-foot-three. This pediatric disease kept Chuck on the children's floor surrounded by wallpaper decorated with Flintstone friends and dinosaurs. He didn't need Santa to add to his discomfort.

Knowing a little more about this young man than I did, the nurse persisted. "You don't have to believe in him," she said kindly, "but

Many special people who volunteer at the University of Chicago Children's Hospital bring comfort and smiles to the children and their families. We are often reminded that those who volunteer have memories that will last a lifetime. Experiencing the struggles and courage of sick children can be a life-altering event. Our volunteers often remark that they get much more than they give.

CHILD LIFE DEPARTMENT, UNIVERSITY OF CHICAGO
CHILDREN'S HOSPITAL

remember that there are lots of little children around here who believe with all their hearts and they're watching you."

"Well, okay," said Chuck reluctantly. "Just make sure he doesn't stay too long."

As I entered the room, I saw a strikingly handsome young man with broad shoulders sitting up in bed. The only thing that gave away

Reflecting back on how the Greater Kansas City Community Foundation has grown and changed, I am reminded of a friend who helped me see the power of individuals to improve the world. Since that fateful meeting in 1989, our Foundation has not been the same. We now are committed to giving donors the opportunity for their personal involvement to touch lives and, in return, have their own lives transformed.

JAN KREAMER, CEO, GREATER KANSAS CITY
COMMUNITY FOUNDATION

his condition was his completely bald head—the result of just finishing six rounds of chemotherapy.

"Hi," I said. "I'm Santa. What's your name, good-looking?"

Chuck looked at me with a flash of anger and hurt in his eyes. Hesitantly, he ran his hand over the top of his smooth head and I realized at once that I'd made a terrible mistake. I had little knowledge or experience with cancer patients and I wasn't equipped to respond the way I should have. However, I did have one thing going for me: I knew a lot about hair loss.

"There are plenty of handsome hunks who don't have any hair on their heads," I told him. "In fact, I look at one every morning in the mirror." With that, I pulled off my hat and curly white wig and exposed my own bald head.

Startled, Chuck laughed aloud and I laughed with him. How wonderful it was to see such a broad smile and hearty laugh from someone who didn't want to see me to begin with and who then felt insulted by the first words out of my mouth. This shared source of embarrassment broke the ice and gave me a chance to get to know a kind person with a great sense of humor.

Chuck told me that losing his hair was a tough thing to accept. In fact, to keep in practice, he shampooed his head every night with his favorite shampoo just like he always did before his chemotherapy. "I'm not going to let this no-hair thing change my routine," he said with a smirk. This kind of fun attitude gave me a sharp picture of the way that a sense of humor allowed Chuck to face what life had handed him. No tears or anger for him—life was too much fun to give up on.

As we talked, I learned that Chuck had a wonderful circle of friends who fed right into his need for laughter. It seems that I was not the first one to make Chuck laugh by baring a bald head. When his hair first began to drop, three of Chuck's friends shaved their own heads and proudly wore their badge of friendship—not in sympathy, but in good humor. Chuck told me he remembered that he had been feeling particularly down about the whole thing when his friends arrived minus their hair. Instantly, they jumped on each other rubbing each other's shiny heads; they laughed until they cried and then they fell into a group hug of support. What a difference a little kindness and a whole lot of laughter make in the way we view the world.

For quite some time, Chuck told funny stories that got bigger and funnier the longer they went on. I saw firsthand that a shared joke, a funny story, and a genuine smile are all priceless gifts. Chuck showed me that laughter and kindness are the secrets to a good and fulfilling life—no matter how long or short that life may be.

In his own way, Chuck taught us that even in the most life threatening of situations, humor is a friend that makes all things bearable. Asking nothing in return, he showed me how to live with any pain or raw deal that life might hand out.

This chapter is dedicated to Chuck Manion: March 12, 1976–May 8, 1997.

POKER FACES

*A*lmost everywhere I went on my hospital rounds, Santa Claus was warmly received. But on one particular day, I stopped to see some troubled teens in a psychiatric ward where Santa was definitely not wanted.

"Go away!" they shouted when they saw me. "We don't need any Santa here!"

Some of these kids were grappling with drug and alcohol addictions; others were struggling with mental and emotional problems that stemmed from broken homes and abusive parents. They had no desire to be part of the holiday hoopla and it was my guess that they believed I was just someone who was superficially motivated by his own need to feel good. They were a tough crew and I didn't know how to break through to them.

First, I tried small talk to penetrate the icy veneer. "Hi, guys," I started with my deepest Santa voice. "How are you today?" They barely glanced at me. "I've brought each of you a gift," I added,

hoping to raise some interest. "Keep your gift, old man," sneered one boy. "We don't need no piece of junk from you." Undaunted, I handed each teen a teddy bear which drew a round of raucous laugher. "Hey look," mocked one girl, "I got a cuddly, little bear who loves me." Then with a look of contempt, she stared me down as she threw her bear against the far wall. All the teens dropped their bears and turned away from me.

I felt defeated. I was the object of mockery and I was uncomfortable, embarrassed, and humiliated. I couldn't be Santa Claus on this ward. Frustrated, I gave up and was making my way to the door when I noticed four guys sitting around a table playing cards.

These were the kind of kids who caused heartaches for parents. Hospital garb had replaced their ratty jeans and cut-off tee shirts, but their body language and steely stares shouted, "Don't mess with me!"

I went over to them and asked what they were playing.

"Poker," muttered one without looking up.

"That's my favorite game," I ventured. "Can you deal me in?"

Another cynic rolled his eyes. "You don't know nothin' about cards," he grumbled.

I always ask people, "Would you be doing this job if you did not need any money?" To do this in our day and age takes integrity of the heart and character of the mind. Working with adjudicated youth—the future of America—out in the Colorado Rocky Mountains has given me a new peace on this earth. To give myself over so completely to one thing requires me to turn my life upside down and inside out for 16 days of every month. It makes it all worthwhile when they ask me, "Why do you keep coming out here?" I tell them, "Because I like your company out here." It feels amazing to get a hug from a kid who probably has not been permitted to display his affection for somebody in years in the facilities. He can squeeze you so hard because he's not seen you in six days, and he's so happy that you have come back and not quit on him. Do not ever quit on anyone or anything. There will always be a chance for a change.

RYAN COMMENT, AGE 24, WORKS WITH

JUVENILE DELINQUENTS THROUGH

ALTERNATIVE YOUTH ADVENTURES IN COLORADO

I stood my ground. "How about this," I asked, challenging them to a bet. "If I lose three out of five games, you can have my hat, beard, and wig. If I win, you get to wish me Merry Christmas and take my teddy bears."

There were whoops and hollers all around. This did, indeed, seem like a ridiculous proposition, especially for a man who doesn't play cards.

"Okay," said one teenager, "but you ain't gonna look much like Santa when we're through with you."

I sat down and reached over my big Santa belly to pick up my cards. In the first hand, I drew three kings and won. The guys accredited my good fortune to their generosity.

I won the second hand with a pair of aces and tens. They attributed this to dumb luck. Just when I thought I wouldn't be forced to walk out of there half-naked after all, I lost the third hand. There were snickers and guffaws all around.

Then, to my own astonishment, and theirs, I won the fourth! I leaned over the table and grinned. "Guess old Santa gets to keep his hat," I laughed.

The teenagers looked at me in disbelief, toothpicks dangling from their lips, cards dropping from their fingers.

I stood up and stretched my legs. "Well," I said. "This means you've got to take those bears off my hands and wish me a Merry Christmas."

"Merry Christmas," they mumbled disgruntled, but I saw hints of smiles begin to creep across their faces. The head psychiatric nurse came up to me and whispered, "I can't believe that!"

"I can't either," I whispered back. "I've never won three hands of poker in my life!"

I haven't played cards again since that day, but that game reinforced an important lesson I had learned years earlier from my own son. He had gone through a couple of difficult years when he was a teen doing everything I had told him for fifteen years he shouldn't do. When he began to come to his senses when he hit nineteen, my son says that the first thing he did was to look around to see if his dad was still there — and he was. He said to me, "I was on the verge of trashing my life and you didn't walk away from me. Thank you." It would have broken my heart to walk away from my son or from those kids in that hospital ward. I hope I'm always willing to take a good-humored gamble on people I think are worthwhile, especially kids.

If you're a dad or a mom, if your kids are teenagers, or if they're five, or if they're thirty-five, make sure you're always willing to give them a smile and a helping hand. That doesn't mean you have to agree with what they're doing, but make sure when they're ready to come back, you're there. That's being philanthropic with your own loved ones — not just with strangers.

ONE LAST STOP

*n*o one enjoys a hospital stay—especially if you're having surgery. It doesn't make any difference if it's a small operation or major surgery; the preparation and anticipation are very stressful. Whether or not you've had this experience yourself, imagine what it must be like for a child who is in the hospital awaiting surgery. The environment is totally unfamiliar. The food is not like mom's. There are weird smells everywhere. In addition, strangers are forever poking and prodding your body in all sorts of places. In some children, the reaction to all this uncertainty shows in their eyes as they open wide in a shaky attempt to "be brave." Others show their feelings in soft, unending sobs, and still others make their feelings very clear with violent screams. It's hard to fathom what goes on in their little minds at such a scary time.

It is rare that Santa is allowed to visit these children because, in the good judgment of the hospital administrators, these patients are already dealing with a volatile mix of emotions and there is much preparatory medical work to be done. However, I vividly remember one late Friday afternoon when Santa was visiting the Children's Medical Center of Dayton, Ohio. Santa and his team were getting ready to leave the hospital (or as I always like to say — going back to the North Pole) when we approached a hallway where a young patient on a gurney was being wheeled toward us. One of the nurses leading the boy's medical team told me that he was going down to surgery so it would be best not to stop and talk. I'm sure this nurse was hoping that Santa would duck out of the way because she had a destination and a timetable, but surely she didn't understand that the presence of Santa is not

something that can be ignored — even by a young man sleepy with the effects of presurgery anesthesia.

At first, I didn't completely disregard the nurse's request. I stood perfectly still as the little group approached. I noticed right away that the gurney was surrounded by anxious members of the boy's family — it looked like mom, dad, grandma, grandpa, and even big sister were

there to lend a supportive hand. As they came closer, I saw their worried faces brighten up as they prodded the boy to wake up.

"Zachary, look! Santa has come to see you before your operation!"

"Zachary, you were worried that Santa wasn't going to get your list before Christmas. Here he is!"

"Zachary, don't fall asleep yet. Here's Santa to see you!"

By the time we met in the middle of the hallway, Zachary was sitting up with sleepy eyes and

Nobody likes to be sick. However, for children, being ill can be especially difficult. Volunteers at The Children's Medical Center of Dayton help soothe children who are in unbelievable pain. For children who are sick, seeing a clown or Santa Claus or receiving a gift gives them a moment to forget their problems. They can be a kid again.

KAREN MULLER,

THE CHILDREN'S MEDICAL CENTER

a huge lopsided grin on his face. This little boy who was about four or five years old was struggling valiantly against the anesthesia to talk to Santa.

"Santa," he said with a wobbly voice, "did you really want to see me before my operation?"

"Zachary," I told him as I laid his head back down and leaned closer, "the elves told me this morning that you were going to be here and that I should come right away to hold your hand for good luck before you go into surgery and to get your Christmas list so they can begin to prepare your Christmas surprises."

To everyone's surprise, despite his groggy state, Zachary began to rattle off his wish list. The list included not only what he wanted for himself, but also what his sister wanted and what he called "a nice idea for Mom and Dad."

As we all laughed, the medical team began to plow forward in their appointed duty and began to push Zachary further down the hall. I held his hand and continued to walk with him a little way.

"I'm going to say a prayer for you, Zachary," I told him as I looked deeply into his half-open eyes. "And I want you to do something for me. On Christmas Eve, be sure to leave out a big plate of cookies and a glass of milk because Santa gets really hungry delivering all those wonderful presents."

Then I stepped back and winked a final goodbye as the gurney picked up speed. Suddenly, I saw Zachary turn back to me as he asked, "What kind of cookies?"

"Chocolate chip!" I yelled down the hall as I watched him wave goodbye and then settle back down.

Zachary may have been two minutes late for his surgery, but it was two minutes well spent, surrounded by people who loved him and I

The most selfish thing you can do is to be selfless.

BILL HALAMANDARIS, PRESIDENT,
HEART OF AMERICA FOUNDATION

was grateful that fate had brought us all together at that moment in time. Later, I thought a lot about Zachary's family who were obviously concerned about his health, but who stood by him with happy and gleeful support all the way down the long corridor. That's the way it should be for every human being. We all need and deserve the support and love of others—especially when we are sick, when we hurt, and when we are afraid. Sadly, there are many people who have no one to offer this basic comfort. For them, each of us can be that other human being who cares. Through our volunteer activities, we can give the one thing that no amount of money can buy, no corporate board can order, and that no other person in the universe possesses—our very own personal time and attention given to those in need. These few moments can give a lonely person a smile—if that seems too simplistic to be important, consider that it may be the only happy experience the person might have all day. Today, tell a joke, make someone smile.

NO TWO KIDS ARE ALIKE

*W*hen visiting sick children, Santa and his helpers often feel an ache of emptiness. You feel so helpless seeing children in pain and not being able to do anything about it. Fortunately, we also have many laughs. The one thing about a Santa visit that most often makes us all laugh out loud is the way the children react to Santa's sudden appearance. Each reaction is different, personal, and often quite funny.

I've looked back over my years as Santa and pulled up some Santa visits that are most memorable. These children (and their parents) have left with me a piece of themselves that will keep me good company the rest of my life. How can I ever feel lonely or depressed when I have such wonderful memories of such beautiful children?

One morning as I walked in the front door of a hospital, the first child I saw was a two-year-old girl who was in the lobby with her mom. I remember her so clearly: She was a beautiful child with long, curly blond hair wearing a lilac-colored ski jacket. As soon as she saw me, she leapt off her mother's lap and literally jumped up and down and up and down clapping her hands and yelling "Santa! Santa!" She ran across the lobby to meet me, jumped up and down again clapping her hands and then turned around and ran back to her mother to again jump up and down and clap her hands. I felt tired just watching this little girl run, jump, and clap back and forth at least four times. She never did stand still long enough for me to talk to her, but there was no doubt she loved her visit with Santa.

Most kids do love Santa—sort of. One little boy who I would guess was about three years old marched right up to my chair and sat on my lap without a moment's hesitation or fear. He was smiling with his whole body and obviously enjoying his moment in the spotlight. When his time was up, he jumped down off my knee and proceeded to give everyone in my entourage a big hug and kiss—the camera operator, the child-life worker, my assistant, and so on. Then he started back toward me, and I figured it was my turn for a kiss. However, my little friend stopped dead in his tracks, took another good look at my long whiskers, thought for a moment, and then blew me a kiss instead. Boy, did everyone laugh at that one!

There's just no predicting what kids will do. One day when I was making the rounds room to room, a little four-year-old named Matthew was watching me carefully as I worked my way down the hall to the room where his baby brother was recovering from surgery. Finally, when I reached his room, he walked right up to me and, standing toe to toe, he looked down at my boots and then up at my head and announced for everyone to hear, "Wow, you're big!" But that fact didn't scare Matthew; it amazed him. Santa bent down, picked the boy up, and received a tight bear hug. It didn't take me long to realize that Matthew had no plans of letting go any time soon. "Okay, Matthew," I said, "time to get down now. Okay, that's a nice big hug, now let me go inside and see your baby brother. Okay, time to stop hugging now." By this time, I was crouched down so Matthew's feet could touch the floor, but he was still holding on tight. As we stood there in this comical predicament, I realized that perhaps because Matthew's ill brother was taking so much of his parents' time and attention, this was one moment that was all for him and he just couldn't bear to let it go.

As much as some kids like Matthew like to get real close to Santa, others think Santa is really great—from afar. One day, I saw a little girl about two years old spying on me from behind her mother's leg. As I came in and out of each hospital room, there she would be about ten feet away watching me. I would wave to her, but she would always retreat to the safe refuge behind her mother. This went on for about a half-hour when I decided to see if I couldn't entice her to come closer. I sat down on the floor in the hallway with my back against the wall and my legs out straight in front of me, hoping that at eye level I wouldn't look so imposing. I had the best belly laugh when I saw that my little shadow immediately sat down also—still about ten feet away. As we all watched with great enjoyment, she very slowly, inch-by-inch, schushed herself along the floor coming closer and closer, stopping about two feet away from me—just close enough to reach for the teddy bear and to get her picture taken with Santa. I'm sure that by next year this is one little girl who will be ready to jump right on Santa's lap—she just didn't want to rush into it this year.

The true joy of being Santa is that you realize that the giving of yourself has universal acceptance and the rewards far outweigh any sacrifice. People have no barriers to gender, age, color, or religion when it comes to accepting kindness and therefore everyone can and should participate in making other lives better in even the smallest ways every day. Santa's Gift is a fantastic vehicle for delivering kindness.

DAVID AND ANDREA GAYNES,
THE JEWISH SANTA AND HIS HELPER

I've seen many, many children who don't mind sitting with Santa—as long as mom or dad (or both) come too. Very often children, especially infants and young toddlers, have no idea who I am or why their parents are handing them over to this very weird looking stranger. Of course, this is scary and I try hard to keep the experience from turning into a nightmare. These hospitalized kids have all had to do enough things that they don't want to do—visiting Santa should not be one more thing added to that list. To keep the visit enjoyable, I always ask the parents of hesitant kids to join us. We all get in the picture and get a hug from Santa. I am always amazed and humbled when I see how much little children look to their parents for information about the world. If it's okay for this big man in the red suit to hug mommy, they reason, then it's okay for me, too.

Of course, this doesn't work with all kids. Some just don't like Santa at all—and there's nothing that will change their mind. As I made my way toward the children's unit, I passed through a patient waiting area and saw a little five-year-old sitting on his dad's lap. "Merry Christmas!" I yelled as I waved to the boy across the room. The boy stared at me for a second or two and then let out a scream of horror. He turned away throwing his arms around his dad's neck for dear life. The more dad tried to convince his son that he should wave to Santa, the louder the boy cried.

"Okay, well, I'll be moving along now," I laughed as we hurried away down the hall. You can't please everyone. About a half hour later, as we followed our guide from one side of the building to the other, we again passed through the waiting area and sure enough, there was our little friend. One look at me returning to the room and he scurried back up on to his dad's lap and again began to howl. Not soft sobs — but loud petrified screams.

"Sorry," I said with a laugh as I passed by the dad. "Most kids don't have such a strong reaction to me." The dad gave me an embarrassed smile and shrugged his shoulders having no idea why his son was so upset. And off we went.

A short while later it was time to take the elevator up to the next floor, and . . . you guessed it: We had to pass by the waiting room and my buddy was still sitting there.

This was just a nightmare for this little boy, but we couldn't help but laugh. All I wanted to do was bring happiness to sick children and here three times in one day I had made the same little boy cry. That must be some kind of record for a Santa. As we prayed the elevator would hurry up and open so this child could calm down again, I turned and saw that although he hadn't eased up on the crying, he was now waving at me and through heaving sobs saying, "Bye Santa." I'll never again underestimate the power of Santa to win over a child—even just a little bit.

Later, I met a young lady about two years old who also wasn't so sure Santa was all he had been cracked up to be, but she was a bit more reserved in her reaction. This child walked up to me and sat herself on my lap. There were no tears and no pulling away but, on her face, she wore a look of absolute repulsion. She knit her eyebrows tightly together. Her jaw dropped down and her mouth opened and she just stared at me as if I were the ugliest thing she had ever seen. Throughout our visit, the look on her face never changed. I laugh to myself every time I picture that cute little face all scrunched up.

The facial expressions, the body language, and the smiles are all part of the wonderful universal language of children. Because children from all over the world come to the great hospitals in the United States, I have sat with families of many nationalities, cultures, and religions and have seen time and time again that even when we speak different languages, the message is quite easily communicated—Santa loves you. I remember a young, beautiful mother who placed her infant on my lap as I sat in the lobby of one hospital. I asked her, "What is your baby's name?" She looked worried, hesitated a moment and then said with what sounded to me like a strong Spanish accent, "No English."

"Oh! Well then," I said as I reached out to hold her hand, "Feliz Navidad!" The woman beamed with joy and began talking in Spanish a mile a minute. I, unfortunately, had already used the only two Spanish words I knew. But she continued on happily as I nodded and stroked the face of her beautiful child. The language of joy is universal.

I also remember a twenty-year-old foreigner who brightened my day. A young woman came rushing up to my Santa chair saying, "Santa, my friend is visiting from Palestine and has never in her life had her picture taken with Santa! Could she sit on your lap?"

"Of course!" I said, but I had to laugh when I saw that like so many kids on their first visit to Santa, she too hung back. This young lady was obviously very unsure about the propriety of sitting on a strange man's lap and knew only one English word to explain: "No." We kept encouraging her until my female assistant showed her how to do it and also showed her that in America it's okay to sit on the lap of the man in the red suit. Shy and hesitant, she approached and sat gently on my knee. She looked toward the camera and gave the most beautiful smile. Everyone around applauded and laughed with shared joy. No matter what the age or nationality, the first picture with Santa is always a special moment.

This young lady's experience with Santa was typical of the challenge I face with the older children. I don't want to embarrass them, but I don't want to leave them out either. One fourteen-year-old waited on line quite a while to see me (probably enticed by the cute teddy bears we were giving away). When it was her turn, she stood in front of me and said, "I want to sit on your lap, but I don't want my picture taken." Well, that's no problem for Santa. "Sure, have a seat," I said patting my knee. The young teen sat down and happily took her teddy bear. After a bit of chitchat, she turned to the cameraman and said, "It's okay. You can take my picture." None of us were at all surprised. Over and over again, teens insist they don't want a picture taken with Santa (just to let us know right up front that they don't want any part of this kid stuff), but then without exception before our visit is over they change their minds.

Sometimes the need to look grown-up starts early. I remember seeing two ten-year-old boys in the playroom. As I walked in, they shot each other a knowing glance that sealed their agreement that they were too cool for Santa and they turned back to their game. But their bravado melted quickly when I sat down to play a few rolls of the dice and before I knew it they were jokingly pushing each other back, fighting to be the first to sit on my lap to get his picture taken. Maybe the hardest part of being a young teen is looking big without giving up the joy that comes with believing in Santa.

My years as Santa have proven to me beyond a doubt that Santa is nothing less than pure magic—for anyone of any age. My recollections of a visit with one young man always remind me of this power. There was a seven-year-old boy on the orthopedic surgical floor who had heard that Santa was in the building. Apparently, he was insistent that his mom take him to find Santa. Finally giving in to his pleas, she walked him down the hall to the elevator and stood waiting for the doors to open. Soon a nurse came by and suggested that they wait in his own room because Santa was going to visit every child in the hospital—they needn't go looking for him. "If you just wait and be good," she told her little patient, "Santa will come to you." No sooner had she made this promise than the elevator door opened and there I

In today's world, if we are to continue our movement toward a civil society, it is so important to keep in mind the three tenets that are inherent in that journey: Opportunity, Responsibility, and Community. Personally, I am not a big fan of the term "giving back," as it could represent the ability for an individual to write a check, attend an event, or simply explore the countless ways to really assist those in the community that are asked to do more with less, or face enormous challenges in their life. A deep and profound commitment to these ideals is more effectively embraced by the notion that those of us who are in the private sector and are blessed "have a duty to understand one's responsibility to our communities." John Gardner, founder of Common Cause stated it best when he said: "Freedom and responsibility, liberty and duty . . . that's the deal."

JONATHAN TISCH, CHAIRMAN AND CEO, LOEWS HOTELS

stood. The child just froze in place with a look of absolute awe on his face. His eyes widened, his mouth dropped open, and he couldn't speak. "Well, hello!" I said. "I've been looking for you!" The boy didn't move. In his short life, this may have been the first time he saw for himself that Santa really is magical. Of course, his mom and the nurse were laughing hysterically at the perfect timing of my appearance—this is one happy moment that I'll bet they both long remember. It wasn't until later that I learned the reason for their laughter, but

I wasn't surprised. I had long ago learned that the hand of fate often makes sure that I am where I should be at the right time.

This belief brings up a question we all have to ask ourselves: Are we where we should be? Or do we ignore the opportunities that come our way to help others? Just like some of the enthusiastic children I see, some adults are excited by the idea of helping others and embrace it with joy, plowing ahead despite any possible fears. However, others, probably the majority of us, hold back. Like the little children who

Community service, which includes philanthropy, is a core value of the American labor movement. Labor believes that human beings have advanced more through having learned the value of cooperative, caring behavior rather than individual cunning and ruthless competition. We encourage our members to give freely of their time and money to community services because the quality of life in their communities is just as important as their jobs. As a result, millions of union members are involved in organizations such as Boy Scouts and United Way. The labor movement, through our members, is committed to setting an example of community leadership by showing others how to care for and to improve the communities where we live and raise our children.

MORTON BAHR, PRESIDENT,
COMMUNICATIONS WORKERS OF AMERICA

watch Santa from afar, we are interested and it's something we want to do, but we're also afraid. We think about it, wait on it, get close, and then change our minds. Giving a piece of ourselves to others is an idea that looks good from far away but when we get up close we put it off until tomorrow.

We laugh when we see children who run away from Santa because we know they want so desperately to sit on his lap, but are afraid of the strangeness of his long white beard and red suit. We know there is nothing to fear, but it's tough to convince a tot who has never tried it. Volunteering is the same: I see people all the time who I know want to help out, but pull back at the strangeness of it. Sometimes I want to act like one of those parents and just pick up the balker and plop him or her down in the middle of it. However, I can't, so I recommend another strategy that I've learned from parents—bring someone along with you for courage. If you take a family member or friend with you to your local hospital, food pantry, clothing drive, blood drive, community walk, or whatever, you might find it much easier and more fun to pitch in. It won't be long before you find that helping others brings you the kind of joy and wonderful memories my little ones have given to me.

Reflection by

NORMAN LEAR

No single individual has had more influence through the medium of television in its 50-year history than Norman Lear. He was a comedy writer for various television programs in the 1950s; a writer-producer for television specials in the 1960s; and creator, producer, and writer for popular television series in the 1970s, including All in the Family, Sanford and Son, Maude, *and* Mary Hartman, Mary Hartman. *During his remarkable career, Lear won four Emmy Awards, was inducted into the Academy of Television Arts and Sciences Hall of Fame (1984), received the Humanitarian Award from the National Council of Christians and Jews, as well as the Distinguished American Award. Lear also founded People for the American Way to defend core First Amendment freedoms, and the Business Enterprise Trust to celebrate businesses that advance the public good while achieving financial success.*

I truly believe that laughter adds time to your life. I just wrote a letter to Mel Brooks thanking him for sending me tickets to see the Broadway play *The Producers*—I know that watching that very funny play has added months, maybe a year of time, onto my life. Through the years, people like Bea Arthur who played the lead in *Maude* and Carroll O'Connor in *All in the Family* have made me laugh so hard that I found crevices in my body I didn't know existed. I've spent so much time laughing through my career that I'm convinced I'll be one-hundred-and-eleven years old before I die. That's the gift these performers and the writers and directors with whom I've collaborated have given to me.

Looking back, I'm proud that I have been able to share that gift with so many others. It doesn't matter how many times I hear an audience laugh at something I've written or produced, I laugh too. I get as I give. If you have ever sat in the middle of a theater at a play or movie where the audience laughs as one, you can see people rise up in the dark and lean forward and then come back into their chairs with this enormous guffaw; it's so deeply spiritual to see that many people enjoying a moment in time together. Even if one person thirteen seats over and three rows in front of me laughs, I just fall in love with that sound—with that person. I may never actually meet that person, but I'll remember that wonderful sound of joy. It's so rewarding. I remember flying across country from Los Angeles to New York one night and looking down and thinking, "It's possible that wherever I see a light I've played a part in making somebody laugh." That's a wonderful feeling.

I think that a concern and empathy for humanity runs directly along with a career that seeks to make others laugh. I've enjoyed working and creating in the not-for-profit arena also. Too often, people who can afford to, miss the fun in philanthropy; they work at it rather than swing with their instincts. Giving freely takes the worry out of philanthropy. Right now, I'm touring an original copy of the Declaration of Independence— the birth certificate of our country. On July 4, 1776, twenty-five copies were created and my family owns one of them. While it was in the capitol building in Salt Lake City, Utah, during the winter Olympics, we watched a hundred thousand people in just one week come into the rotunda to view this document. Teachers came up to me with tears in their eyes saying they had always dreamed of taking their classes to Washington, D.C., to see documents like this but could never raise the money. They thanked us over and over for giving their students this opportunity. There's no way to quantify how we felt. Giving nurtures the giver and it's fun.

PART III

Stories *of* HOPE

A Handful of Preemies

A Little Heart Goes a Long Way

A Smile of Hope

Blow Me a Kiss

Reflection by Reverend Craig McElvain

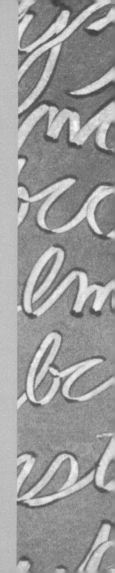

A HANDFUL OF PREEMIES

*n*o matter how many times I visit a neonatal intensive care unit, I will never cease to be amazed by these tiny premature babies lying in man-made wombs called incubators. At first, I found this unit intimidating. It is not a dimly lit, quiet place with soft lullabies gently putting little babies to sleep. It is bright, humming with activity, and wrapped up in all sorts of high-tech monitors, wires, and tubes.

On one particular visit, I stopped to gaze in awe at a tiny baby isolated in his plastic box. He had wires attached to his chest, intravenous tubes going into his head and navel, and tubes from the respirator going into his nose. It was apparent that the daily routine of this little boy did not revolve around only the usual changing of diapers, feeding, and playing. As I stared, an alarm sounded on his monitor and I can tell you that Santa's cherry-red cheeks went pale with fright. The young mother standing nearby laughed, reached in, gave her baby's foot a little jostle, and offered me comfort in my panic as the alarm ceased. "The same thing happened on the first day I came to see Bobby in here," she said. "I was nervous to begin with when all of a sudden, this awful shrill sound started screaming from one of the monitors and a red light was flashing—just like that one was. I thought Bobby was in some kind of terrible trouble and I felt so helpless

because I couldn't do anything for him. However, none of the nurses seemed at all upset. I remember, I grabbed one of them and started yelling at her to do something to help my baby. I guess I expected her to call in some kind of medical SWAT team, but instead she just tapped the bottom of his foot a few times to remind him to keep breathing. The alarm and the light stopped and I had my first embarrassing lesson in how to handle what the doctor calls a common case of apnea." The scare I had is funny when I look back on it now, but because many of these infants are so desperately ill, even today after many more visits to neonatal units I find that the alarms still get my heart pumping with concern.

Well, after my first lesson on the common preemie breathing problem of apnea, I looked around and wondered how I could contribute anything of value here. The nurses were very pleasant to me and didn't seem to mind working around my large presence but these little babies were not yet ready to draw strength from Santa. Then one resourceful staff member, who saw me standing around looking a bit at odds with myself, turned the occasion into an opportunity for these miracle babies and their moms to have their first pictures taken with Santa Claus. Most new parents record their baby's first Christmas with this traditional photo—why shouldn't these parents have a picture, too?

I was escorted ceremoniously to a rocking chair in the corner and the nurse placed a bundle containing a fragile life into my arms. This pint-sized child fit snugly into the crook of my elbow as her sleepy head peeked out of the blankets. So many thoughts ran through my mind as I admired her tiny features. In just her first few weeks of life, she'd had to overcome the odds and tackle the hurdle of survival. Already she had overcome great obstacles. Who knew what life had in store for her, I thought, but thanks to the knowledge and dedication of the people in this unit, she would have a life to look forward to.

In her peaceful slumber, my first little baby seemed oblivious to the commotion and the photographer's flashbulbs as she sucked on her minuscule thumb—but her mom was beaming with happiness. She told me that she had undergone two prior miscarriages and so the early birth of this child was especially frightening. "The first few weeks were the hardest," she told me. "My husband and I couldn't even hold her. All we could do was put our arm through the porthole in the incubator and stroke her head or arm. I've never been so scared in my life. The only thing that kept me from panicking was watching her little arms and legs as they were kicking wildly in the air. From the moment I saw that, I knew she wasn't going to die. And now," she said as her eyes brimmed with tears and her voice broke, "I can hardly believe that here she is sitting on Santa's lap posing for her first Christmas picture. Thank you, Santa, for giving us this wonderful memory."

As we talked, I told her that I understood all too well the fear of losing the child you've finally been given. Emotions I thought were long buried and forgotten came flooding back to me. My own daughter was also born prematurely. After one difficult miscarriage, my wife finally gave birth three months early to a two-pound baby girl who was so small I could hold her entire body in the palm of my hand. When she was born in 1974, the survival rate for preemies was very low, so it was truly a miracle that she survived at all. "Today," I told this hopeful mother, "she is a twenty-eight-year-old healthy woman with a bright future. And that is what I expect you too will have twenty-eight years from now."

Before I left the unit, I had one more photo request from a mom who had just arrived and was glad she hadn't missed her chance to pose with Santa and her *three* babies. The picture was one of those classics:

The happy mother sat in the rocker, her triplets were arranged in her arms, and Santa sat next to her holding three "I Am Loved"® bears. As we sat there laughing over the logistics of propping up three sleepy babies and three floppy bears, I was struck by the amount of love we give to these precious, helpless infants with so much potential. There is no feeling person alive who would not give them all the love and attention they need to grow both physically and psychologically strong.

All the money and knowledge at our disposal can't always ease suffering. Pain is an inextricable part of humanity. But so is love. And like countering balances on a scale, one can lessen the impact of the other. Compassion does more than we give it credit for to not only alleviate emotional suffering but help physical healing. Love reaches a place that medicine cannot, the spirit. And a calm spirit frees the body to heal if it can, or to accept if it cannot. Modern medicine and the feats doctors accomplish are vital to wellness, but let us not forget or ignore the persistent nudging of kindness. A word, a look, a touch has the ability to soothe the distraught, strengthen the weak, and embolden the fearful. Compassion, like a balm for the spirit, is an essential part of treating a patient. The one-pound preemie that lays entwined in plastic tubing and trembling with fragility needs the astute mind of her doctor and the skilled hands of her nurses to survive. But she also needs to be cradled in the sense of her mother's touch.

KRISTEN COMMENT, AGE 28, BOSTON UNIVERSITY—MASTER'S PROGRAM

Why is it then that while we can so easily adore babies, we struggle to love grown-ups? In other units in this very same hospital (or in any hospital anywhere), there are teen throwaways who nobody wants anymore. There are neglected and forgotten elderly. There are mentally challenged patients with no one to turn to. There are addicts who no longer care about the future. So many people all over the country are waiting for someone who will spend some time, offer some love, and see them simply as the human beings they are. What's the difference between these grown people and those little babies?

I think that one reason adults in need are harder to love grows from a perceived lack of hope. In babies, there is bountiful hope that each one will grow to be strong, healthy, and happy. Even the parents of the sickest preemie who is battling the odds hold on for dear life to the slimmest thread of hope. Can we feel that same hope for sick or neglected adults? I think we can if we take the time to look into their eyes where we'll see the small child who once looked out at the world with trust and expectation. Sharing an afternoon with those in need of companionship and comfort can plant again that seed of hope. Who knows how large it will grow.

A LITTLE HEART
GOES A LONG WAY

It was late afternoon when Santa left the hospital and closed the doors to his van behind him. In the privacy of the van with its darkened glass, Santa removed his hat and beard to relax for a few moments before moving on to the next hospital. The adrenaline rush from these hospital tours was an incredible thing. I had just met with about 250 children who tugged, laughed, jumped, and hugged all day long. Yet I was still feeling excited about moving on to the next hospital where more children were waiting. As my assistant drove, I closed my eyes letting my head swarm with visions of children of every size and color and disposition, yet all so very much the same in their love of Santa. What was it, I wondered, about this big man in his red suit? Why did children throw aside their pain to hug him? Why did they ignore the pleas of the nurses to stay in their beds to run to his side?

Why do children who are so miserable with their illness and in their separation from their parents brighten up with glee at the first glimpse of this rotund mythical man? I just couldn't put my finger on what it was that ignited such a spontaneous and unreserved reaction in all these children.

Well, there was no more time to wonder as we pulled into the parking lot of our next stop—Rush-Presbyterian-St. Luke's Medical Center in Chicago. A quick wipe of the brow as I replaced my hat and beard, a swig of water, and a little more rouge on the cheeks, and we were ready to go.

As we entered the hospital, the nurses and staff greeted us with warm hospitality. "How many children are in this hospital today?" I asked our guide. "About 150," she said. "Now if you follow me this way, I'll bring you to the intensive care unit where there are only about 35 children expecting to see you." I nodded and followed her along the hall knowing that before the day was over I would see all 150 children. I'm not quite sure how it works, but we had found that there is some

That's the beauty of giving: The gifts I receive far outweigh the gifts I am able to give.

KIMBERLY WILLIAMS, ACTRESS

kind of incredible networking system in hospitals that spreads the news of Santa's arrival to every young person under its roof within 30 minutes of our arrival. And every one of them was sure that Santa would soon stop by with his cheery "ho-ho-ho!"

But first things first. I knew that a pediatric intensive care unit offers many challenges to a visiting Santa. It's not always a good place to be loud and joyous. Some children are too ill to even know he is there; others are too medicated to react to his hug; and there are others who in their

ARTWORK BY MARY

excitement will dislodge monitoring wires and tubes to get close to him. (Never a favorite occurrence for these hard-working nurses.) Therefore, I knew that each child had to be approached with care and caution. However, I didn't know that in this particular unit there was a young boy named Demetri whose desire to see Santa would be so great, that I would have to break some rules just to give him a hug.

Six-year-old Demetri had received a heart transplant four days earlier and was separated from the world in a glass-walled isolation room. He could see everything going on in the hall and the nurses and doctors could see him, but the room was basically sealed off and germ-free. As I approached his room, the nurse warned me that all I could do for Demetri was wave to him through the glass. As I peered in, I saw a frail little boy lying on his back with his eyes closed. His complexion was exceptionally pale in contrast to the long, dark eyelashes that lay against his sunken cheeks. His small body seemed lost among the intricate tangle of medical tubes and wires that hooked his body to life-saving monitors. How wonderful, I thought, that we have the technology and the expertise to save this child's life; yet how frightened he must be all alone in that room.

Then, as if feeling my presence, Demetri opened his eyes and turned toward me. At first his eyes widened and then his face, that had just seconds before seemed so sickly, glowed with an open-mouthed smile that filled the room and the distance between us. I gave him a hearty wave that I hoped would cheer him — without realizing the kind

It takes a special kind of person to volunteer their time to help out in the community, particularly in a hospital setting. In fact, the qualities that make a good volunteer are many of the same qualities that make a good health care worker: dedication, compassion, initiative, a genuine interest in other people, and a big heart. Volunteers help Rush provide the highest quality health care, and the joy and comfort they bring to Rush patients and families—through good deeds both large and small— is beyond measure.

LARRY J. GOODMAN, M.D., PRESIDENT AND CEO,
RUSH-PRESBYTERIAN-ST. LUKE'S MEDICAL CENTER

of reaction it would spark. Demetri sat straight up and began to wave his arms wildly. "Santa!" he yelled. "Santa!"

One of the nurses jumped to attention and ran into Demetri's room to try to calm him down, but to no avail. He pulled away from her and reached his thin arms out to me. "I want to see Santa," he cried. Demetri's diseased heart had made him feel weak and so very sick his whole young life, but now he had a new heart that was beating with excitement and new life, while I just stood there frozen, not knowing what to do. I couldn't walk away from this little boy who was pleading with me to stay. The gift of love needs to be delivered in person. It's not just the marvels of modern medicine, but also the human touch that heals the heart. But I also knew it might be harmful to his health if I were to follow my instinct to charge into his room, scoop him up in my arms, and hug him until all the pain and fear were gone.

Just as the nurse motioned for me to move on so she could calm him down, a distinguished-looking man in his fifties came up beside me. "It's okay," he said. "I think you should stay." From the way he was looking at Demetri, I knew this must be the cardiologist. "Santa," he said, "we're doing a lot of wonderful things here at the hospital to give Demetri a new life, but I'm not sure that keeping him separated from you is going to help him recover any better. Why don't you wait here for a few minutes and the nurse and I will see if we can bring Demetri to you." The hallway was suddenly hushed in total silence. This had never been done before and I could see that the nurses were both excited by the idea and worried at the same time.

We all watched in apprehensive silence as the doctor and nurse ever so carefully lifted Demetri from his bed into a small carriage with all of his supporting equipment still hooked onto a rolling rack. We were collectively holding our breath hoping this move wouldn't upset the healing process—the incision was still very sore and his muscles were weak, and his heart was still adjusting to its new home. But at the same time, we were feeling the contagious effect of Demetri's broad smile. He never took his eyes off me and he never for a second indicated that maybe this wasn't a good idea. Apparently, Demetri would endure anything to see Santa up close and for real.

As Demetri was wheeled out of the isolation room, I took only one hesitant step toward him. I was afraid my furry suit and shaggy beard might somehow contaminate this child who just days earlier had received a new heart. However, Demetri had no such worries. He wanted a no-holds-barred hug from Santa and nothing was going to stop him. Again, he reached out his arms inviting me to touch his life. I walked closer, knelt down, and embraced this beautiful, courageous

To give, to acknowledge another's existence, acknowledges our own. It acknowledges our common bond as living beings. It acknowledges that we journey together. It acknowledges the unique struggle that each of us has as humans, that all of us share in this life. It allows us to experience our compassion for each other and for ourselves. When we do that, we open our hearts and know love. When we know love, we know why we exist.

PAUL MICHAEL GLASER, DIRECTOR/PRODUCER

child. My own heart beat faster and my tears of gratitude spilled onto my rouged cheeks.

As I knelt at his side and felt the grip on his thin fingers on my back, I realized that Demetri had given me the answer to the question that I had been thinking about earlier. He showed me that the reason all kids put aside their pain and their discomfort and their fears when they see Santa is that he is a very large symbol of hope that they can physically hold on to. He reminds them of days past when they were healthy and at home. He offers them tangible hope that those days will soon return. The joy of this hope in Demetri's hug was transformed to a renewal of my own profound sense of hope for the return of good health to all hospitalized children.

I am fortunate to be in a position to help other people. But I work with college students all across the country who prove that you don't need to be a celebrity to make a profound difference in someone's life. All you have to do is care.

SCOTT WOLF, ACTOR

A SMILE OF HOPE

I'm an inquisitive sort of Santa. As I walk down the corridors of a hospital, I want to poke my head around the corner or look in a room. The child-life people get a big kick out of that inquisitiveness, but are also very careful to tell Santa that there are some rooms he just can't visit. Children who are too sick aren't in the mood to spend time with Santa and I always try to respect that. Therefore, Santa passes by. Occasionally, there will be a family who does not observe Christmas and Santa always wants to be sensitive to that also. However, in the majority of the rooms, Santa is welcomed and that makes me feel great. Then, there are those few situations where Santa is given the option of whether or not he wants to visit a child. It may be a situation where the hospital and child-life people are trying to be sensitive to Santa if the child's circumstance is one of trauma or great emotion.

I remember on one particular day the child-life person hesitated outside the door of one room and shaking her head she said, "Santa,

I really don't think we have to go into this room because the young man is in a coma and he won't know you're there."

"Well," I said, "I still sometimes just like to stand at the edge of the bed and say a few words of encouragement, maybe even whisper a prayer."

"But," she persisted, "This might be really hard even for Santa. This is a young man named James in his early twenties; he's dying of AIDS and probably has just a few days left."

I thought to myself for a second and then I said, "I would like to go and just spend a couple of minutes with James."

I entered the room, walking very slowly, trying to be quiet and respectful. I immediately noticed that the boy's mother, with graying hair and thin stature, was standing at the bottom of his bed. "I'm Santa," I said softly. "Can I come in and be with your son for just a few minutes?"

She looked at me with empty eyes and despite the look of pain and dismay on her face she said, "Santa, come in if you would like." And she stepped aside to give me more room.

As I moved closer to the bed, I was quickly reminded how AIDS ravages the body. Here lay a young man in his early twenties, now

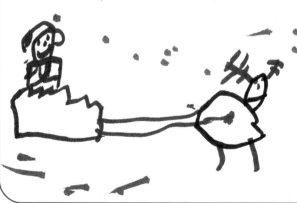

> *Giving is the key that unlocks the door to happiness and fulfillment. Helping others pleases the heart of God. The more you give, the more you receive in return. Jesus Christ said, "Give, and it will be given to you." That is a promise from a living God.*
>
> DR. RUSSELL E. CADLE, FRIENDSHIP MINISTRIES FOUNDATION

weighing 50 — maybe 60 — pounds, almost skeletal, no longer breathing on his own, hair all but gone. I found myself at a loss for words. What could anyone, even Santa, say in the face of this kind of suffering?

As I turned to the boy's mother, I prayed that I would find words that could offer some degree of comfort. "James might not hear me this afternoon," I began hesitantly, " but you can listen to what I have to say for him. I want to remind you that in this world, even in the presence of this kind of tragedy, there is hope."

Shaking her head sadly, she looked at me as large teardrops began to drip down her face. "Santa," she began to cry, "I don't believe there is hope anymore." Then this heartbroken mother took two small steps toward me, put her arms around me, and resting her head on my shoulder, she wept.

As she released her pain in the tears that soaked my red coat, I encouraged her to cry it out. However, I also promised her that God would give her the strength she needed to persevere. "We have to persevere," I told her, "so that our loved ones can live on inside of us. It's in our willingness to wake up each morning, holding on to those wonderful memories, that we can hope to find some spiritual meaning and value in even this kind of incomprehensible loss."

I don't know how long we stood there together, but I know it was long enough for my little hallway contingent to drift down the hall to give us privacy. Only the child-life worker stayed behind and discretely stood at the door to offer her assistance if needed.

Then James' mother began to release her hold on me and she took one small step back; placing both of her hands on my shoulders she said, "You really are Santa!"

I've learned a great deal about the human spirit. I've seen people who have shown great determination, creativity, and generosity to help others. I've also learned about the tremendous courage of people who've been unfortunate victims of ill health or poverty. They've often worked very, very hard to overcome their situation or simply continue to carry their burden with a wonderful, positive attitude.

DON SODO, PRESIDENT AND CEO,
AMERICA'S CHARITIES

"Yes, I really am," I said in my best Santa voice, "and this Santa's one wish this Christmas is that you never give up hope in life."

With a reluctant nod of her head, she looked up at me and smiled—it was a slow-to-form, weak, and uncertain smile—but it was a smile. I took my white-gloved hands and wiped the tears from her cheeks as she said, "Thank you, Santa."

"Thank you," I countered, "for being such a wonderful mom to James for all these years."

As I left the room looking a bit wearier than when I had entered, the child-life worker gently patted me on the shoulder. "Santa," she said, "James' mom has been here at the hospital every day for the last 90 days. Before this moment, I never saw her smile."

No one could bring that young man back to good health—it was, like many life situations, a hopeless circumstance beyond our control. Still, in his mother's simple smile grew the power of hope. Even in times of great sorrow, the poet's conviction is true—Hope does spring eternal from the human heart.

BLOW ME A KISS

*I*t wasn't until I became Santa that I began to understand the different kinds of care that pediatric hospitals provide for young people. If you take a one-day tour of a large hospital, you'll first see the inpatient units where the children are admitted for overnight care. Here you'll find oncology units where the staff treats different kinds of cancers. You'll see infectious disease and respiratory units where you'll need to wear a surgical mask to avoid contamination. (Santa looks especially comical with a surgical mask pulled over his big white moustache and beard!) You'll also find a burn unit, the intensive care unit, and in many hospitals a trauma unit where they care for children who have suffered from serious accidents. Then there is the neonatal care unit for tiny preemies, many of whom are confined to incubators. In addition, often you'll find a special unit for permanently disabled or terminally ill children. Most hospitals also have outpatient clinics that are usually either adjacent to the hospitals or close by. In the outpatient clinics, you'll find children who come just on that one day to have routine checkups, follow-up visits, and/or get their medication. My goal when I visit any hospital is to meet with every single child in every unit. I don't want to miss even one.

There is one other unit found in larger hospitals; it is called the day-hospital unit. Here among other ill children, you'll find young people living with cancer who come in for the day to get chemotherapy and/or radiation treatments. These families have faced the most unthinkable suffering. They have felt the word *cancer* reach in through their ribcage and rip out their heart. It is here that raw hope lives—the kind that is exposed, open, and sometimes painful. Yet, it is also here where the true value of hope is uncovered.

This unit is quite different from other floors in a hospital. The children come in to spend three or four hours hooked up to machines that perform life-saving functions. Some come every day, others every other day, and still others just once in a while.

When I first entered the day-hospital at Children's Memorial Medical Center in Chicago at the end of a long day on my Santa tour, I saw along a large windowed wall big comfortable chairs placed one after the other next to the necessary medical equipment. There were about a dozen kids, fully dressed in their street clothes lounging in the chairs while hooked up to their machines. Some were gabbing with their parents. Others were engrossed in handheld electronic games. Some of the older kids passed the time talking to each other.

Although each and every one of these children has a place in my heart, it was my privilege that day to meet three very special young ladies who I will long remember. As soon as I entered the unit, I saw two teenage girls who had pushed their chairs closer together to pass the time chatting while receiving chemotherapy. The nurse told me that both had been fighting their cancers for several years, going in and out of remission, so this place unwittingly had become a part of their lives. At first, I got the typical teenage reaction to Santa Claus...

People who are involved in charitable causes often have the opportunity to witness the very worthwhile services that their involvement makes possible. That's an important thing, but it isn't quite the same as walking in the shoes of those who truly need the services. The reality for all of us is that it's a short distance from lending a hand to needing the help of others. And when you experience what it's like on the other side, you never come back the same person. "It could be us" is always in the backs of the minds of those who give. Extending ourselves to aid others is always the right thing to do. For all of us.

JOHN EYLER, PRESIDENT AND CEO, TOYS "R" US

"Oh no!" said Sue as she saw me approaching.

"You gotta be kidding!" laughed Kris.

Both hid their faces in their hands as they giggled and laughed. I pulled up a little chair between the two and gave them my best ho-ho-ho! "Look what Santa has for you," I said as they both looked up to see their "I Am Loved"® bears. Because most teenage girls can't resist these huggable gifts, I hoped this would get their attention—it did. The conversation after that was easy and fun. We talked about what most teen girls talk about—boys, school, the latest movies and celebrities, and why mom insists on an early curfew. "These girls are just like my own daughter was at their age," I thought to myself. But on another level, they were so different. At their young age, they have to deal with

the most unfair of circumstances. They have to battle for survival. They have to face their humanness when other teens are allowed to go on feeling invincible. They wake up every morning with the hope that this will be the day that someone will find a cure for their cancer. I'm quite sure that this is the hope that keeps them going and allows them to giggle and gossip and look forward to tomorrow.

As I reached the far end of this unit, I came upon a glass-enclosed room that held two beds and the full array of oncology equipment. These beds, I was told, are usually used by very young children who can't be expected to sit still in a chair for several hours during treatment. In the bed closest to the door, I saw a little two-year-old angel named Rachael. Before we entered, the nurse told me that just before her second birthday Rae-Rae (as she is affectionately called by the staff) was diagnosed with neuroblastoma—an aggressive and threatening childhood cancer. Today she was having her stem cells harvested during a four-hour procedure that linked her to a machine. (Imagine keeping a two-year-old still for four hours!) After high-doses of chemo, she would get three stem cell transplants. Up to this point, she had already had eight rounds of chemo and had lost all her beautiful, dark curls. But, still, she was one of the most beautiful children I had ever seen.

Rachael was sitting up in the hospital bed with crayons and papers around her and with her mom at her side. When she looked up and saw Santa, her face simply beamed. She gave me a smile that literally went from ear to ear and filled the entire room with joy. This was a little girl who obviously did not let her poor health interfere with her enjoyment of life. After taking pictures, sharing some giggles, and hugging the bear, I turned to leave Rachael and move on. As I walked through the door, I turned back for one last look just in time to see little Rachael, so full of awe, surprise, and absolute glee, blow me a kiss. This one second in time reminded me of why I do this. This one kiss was aimed straight for my heart and it hit with unforgettable force. As I looked over and saw her mom trying not to cry, I too felt my eyes well with tears. But, surprisingly, they were not tears of grief, but rather of joy. How could anyone look at this happy child and not feel the power of hope for a healthy tomorrow?

Later, I had the opportunity to speak with Rachael's mom, Diana. "Thank you," she said. "When you're so little and hooked up to machines so often, you don't get a lot of purely magical moments like that. In fact, although we try, it's very hard to create happy memories

Two words. Don't go. It's overtime, bonus, and vacation all rolled into one. Thank you Children's Memorial Medical Center for giving me the opportunity to volunteer, to be a part of your family, to be trusted with your young patients, and to make a difference. What did you say? Don't go! No, I plan to be around for as long as I can make a difference.

MARSHALL CORDELL—VOLUNTEER,
CHILDREN'S MEMORIAL MEDICAL CENTER

when you spend so much time in the hospital. My daughter will not be going to the mall to see Santa like other children so this was especially wonderful. I'll always remember seeing her light up like that; it was priceless to me."

I can't help but be deeply touched when I learn that such a small gesture on my part, just a few moments of my time, has meant so much. It is I who am grateful to Rachael and her mother. As Diana continued to talk I saw, as I had seen so many times before, the strength and courage that parents muster when their children are in need. "When the doctors told me what was wrong with Rachael," she said, "I felt like I was going to die. I have two older boys who I love dearly, but she is my dream baby girl. As a parent, you're so filled with agony you could choose not to get out of bed, but I wake thinking, 'What can I do to make this day a good one for her?' If I can fill her heart with joy every single day and make her happy, I've done as much as a mother can do in this circumstance. And today, it was especially nice to get a little help from Santa."

After some reflection, Diana added, "Hope is the only thing that gets me through each day. We're doing all that can be done medically and then I put it in God's hands. I have people all over the world praying for Rachael and I have placed all my hopes in the power of prayer."

This little girl teaches us the uplifting and positive power of hope. How can any of us say "I can't" when we think of this child and her family who believe that with God's help they can do anything? I know that because of my visit with Rachael I now have the strength to do things in my life that I didn't think I could do before. That is a priceless gift.

I have a very selfish reason to get so involved in the fight against AIDS . . . my 12 year old brother Ricky. I will do whatever I can to help him, and kids like him, beat this disease. I feel blessed that I'm in a position to help get the word out.

KIM WEBSTER, ACTRESS

Reflection by

REVEREND
CRAIG MCELVAIN

Reverend Craig McElvain is Pastor of Heartland Community Church in Overland Park, Kansas. In his ministries, he often works with people in need of comfort. Here is his reflection on why people of faith always have the support and promise of hope.

The philosopher Francis Schaeffer has said that we live in the culture of despair. This is a place where there is no hope — where over and over we hear that the world is going to the proverbial hell in a hand basket. The conservatives are telling us that we're on the eve of destruction because of moral ruin, and the liberals paint a distressing picture of ecological and social ruin. Well, that begs the old question once asked by an evangelist, "Why polish brass on a sinking ship?" If all is already lost, why look around for some promise of hope?

This is where faith comes in. People of faith know that there is hope on two levels: There is hope now for a miracle because God does sometimes poke His head into this world to answer our prayers. There is that possibility of asking for and receiving drastic and unexplainable change. We've seen so many examples of miracles achieved through faith that we hold on to this possibility as long as possible. This is what helps us get up in the morning and face whatever tragedy or crisis life has handed us.

However, it is also true that many times our hope must lie in the hereafter for the kingdom of God is not here in its fullness yet. When someone asks me, "Will you pray for my daughter who is dying?" I pray and believe in the possible power of prayer, but I also know that our real hope is not in this life. This is where the concept of heaven makes a critical comeback. There are many times that I pray for a child who does not get well. I can't explain why God did not show Himself in that case, but I can say with absolute conviction that God gives eternal life to those who trust Him, based on His grace. This is our hope. Paul in his letter to the Corinthians has told us that if we have hope only in this life, we of all people are to be pitied. Ultimately, we have to believe that the day will come, as the Book of Revelations says, when God will wipe away every tear.

I'm reminded of this so often at funerals when people come to me in their grief and ask why God did not answer their prayers. How can they have hope in a joyful tomorrow if they have been let down by their God? They forget that Jesus too wept at the death of his friend Lazarus. They forget that Jesus himself faced the pain and humiliation of death. Jesus too felt sadness and outright anger. He is not a distant observer of human suffering. He knows how we feel when we cry out, "Why?" This creates hope in me when I remember that Jesus too had these feelings and that it's appropriate to be sad and it's okay for me to be mad. My faith also comforts me with the strength of hope because I know that as Jesus rose Lazarus from the dead and as he Himself rose from his tomb, he will raise me to eternal life. This fills me with great hope in any circumstance.

This is not to suggest that people facing personal tragedy who put their faith in God feel less pain. They know their situation stinks; they know they feel very angry and sad. But they have a sense that this won't end here. They know that the dead in Christ will rise and experience a newness of life. Unfortunately, in our busy, affluent lives we forget—until a time of crisis. Then we want someone to tell us there is still hope. More-over, the most remarkable aspect of this faith-based hope is that it is free. It comes with the belief that God's participation in this world's suffering did indeed buy hope for us. But I've noticed that people have trouble accepting this idea of "free" hope. Many feel they need to earn God's help. "What can I do," they ask me, "to get back into God's good graces?" Nothing at all, I tell them. God never left your side. All any of us need to do is to accept God into our lives.

There is something rejuvenating about giving hope to others. Each time I leave a person who is grieving, my own sense of hope increases a hundred fold. When I reach out to someone else who is suffering, it forces the issue of hope on me. It makes me examine if I really believe this stuff myself. My "yes" gets stronger when I'm in the midst of other people's suffering. When John says, "We are the children of God, provided we suffer with Him," he meant it. When Jeff Comment visits the children in the hospital, he chooses to participate in suffering that's not his. That is why he is so richly rewarded. When we choose to suffer with others, we gain a greater sense of hope in our own lives. We become the recipient of an outpouring of hope—and surprisingly of joy, too.

It's a myth that people suffering have no joy; I believe that the opposite is true. I think there is more joy in Harlem than there is in Beverly Hills. Joy is not incompatible with suffering—they often go hand-in-hand. Even in the Bible, most of the passages on rejoicing are in the midst of great suffering. Part of Jeff's rewarding experience has been the incredible joy he has felt by giving a part of himself to people who are going through extremely difficult times.

Yet, sometimes we shield ourselves from other people's suffering because we're afraid joy won't be there. However, my experience has shown me that that's really where joy is. That's where we learn what's really important. If we keep turning away from people and circumstances where we have an opportunity to give and receive hope, selfishness takes over and we fall back into the default lifestyle. Receiving from giving is how God has created the universe. He has told us that if we want to find our life we have to lose it. You may begin helping others with reluctance and uncertainty, but you will soon find that the experience takes nothing from you—it gives to you and fills you with the real meaning of life.

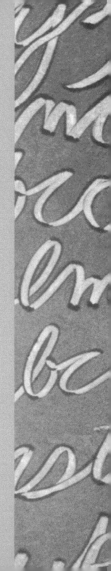

PART IV

Stories of
LOVE

Lucky in Love
A Child Is Lost
The Outpatient Clinic
The Joy of Teamwork

Reflection by Bill Belfiore

LUCKY IN LOVE

*E*ven though Santa is known to have a great deal of stamina, by the tenth day of our tour the wear and tear of traveling across the country, carrying armloads of gifts, and walking miles of hospital corridors, was beginning to take its toll. The suit was now a little worn and shiny in a few spots and there were places that needed repair where too many kids nuzzled a little too hard. Even Santa's beard was getting a little frazzled. But there was no time to rest or tidy up. There was less than one week left before Christmas, so this last visit at St. Christopher's Hospital for Children in the historic city of Philadelphia had to be met with the same kind of enthusiasm shared with the first.

By midday we had already met with about 100 children and fatigue was pushing Santa to the brink of exhaustion. Just as I was about to beg for a rest, I remembered the pediatric head nurse saying, "Santa, I know you're tired, but before you take a break there's one special four-year-old who I think needs a hug right away."

As we walked down the hall, she told me about a little boy named Ryan. Ryan had not been feeling well since around Thanksgiving time. He had been on a series of antibiotic treatments, but was feeling worse by his fourth birthday on December 7. Four days later, his family learned that Ryan had a cancerous brain tumor. Now on December 19,

Ryan was preparing for the very risky surgery that would remove the tumor. She told me that the survival rate after surgery was 65 percent over five years. Although Ryan did not know these details, he knew he was sick and he knew he did not want to be in the hospital on Christmas. The nurse told me that little Ryan was unhappy and angry and that he missed his dog Lucky.

As I listened, I looked ahead and saw a little boy with light blonde tousled hair standing in the hallway with his nurse. This was

Ryan. Even from a distance, I could see that he was very thin, probably down at least a third of his body weight and extremely pale—the kind of pale that told you he was in pain and enduring serious sickness. Yet, his outward signs of illness did not mask the joy that exploded from this child when he caught sight of Santa coming toward him. In his rumpled pajamas, Ryan pulled away from his nurse and began to walk toward me. Then he began to take strong strides as his smile grew larger and larger. Then an interesting thing happened. The pace for both of us began to quicken—we just wanted to get to one another as fast as we could. At last, he broke into a run and I dropped to one knee so I could catch him in my arms as he literally threw himself into my chest and nuzzled his head into my beard.

I remember as I caught this young man and held him in an embrace how all the chatter, the noise of the gurneys, and all the normal sounds

It is hard for anyone to be hospitalized but especially difficult for children. Many times patients are missing friends and family while they are in the hospital. Having special visitors come to see the children makes them feel extra special. Receiving presents makes it even better and getting the "I Am Loved"® bear provides that special smile.

CANDY NYCE, ST. CHRISTOPHER'S HOSPITAL FOR CHILDREN

usually heard on the hospital floor came to an eerie silence. The moment was filled with the quiet of a child who needed the magic of a miracle and a Santa who came to make it seem possible.

I knelt in the hall for a long time with Ryan in my arms. I let him hold on as long as he needed to. I knew that sometimes what these young kids needed most was a long-lasting hug, just to be reassured that they are loved. And who can give away love more freely than the man with the red suit?

Finally, Ryan lifted his head up and looked at me, still beaming with happiness and still holding tightly to my red furry coat. Our eyes caught one another's and again, for what seemed to be a long spell, we just looked with no words being spoken.

At that same time, Ryan's parents rounded the corner and stood at a distance watching their son hold tight to this stranger who had given him back his smile. I later learned that Ryan's parents had just left a very tearful and upsetting meeting with the oncologist who offered them no false hope for their son's recovery. "I thought my heart would break," remembers his mom. "I was so upset and emotionally drained when I headed toward Ryan's room that day. My world was filled with thoughts of surgery, pain, and possibly losing my son. I didn't think I could take another breath without collapsing in grief. Then I looked up and saw Ryan smiling and hugging Santa and my heart just swelled with thankfulness and for the first time in weeks—real joy. Thank God, I thought, for Santa. Thank God that miracles do happen."

When Ryan finally released his grip, I asked him how Lucky was doing. Ryan's jaw dropped in awe at the proof that Santa really

I learned the meaning of life at sixteen.

Alone in the freezing waters of Lake Michigan, my life ebbed. Tossed by a storm, I lost my boat, too far from shore. My heart slowed as I learned what's important. It isn't how popular you are or the things you own that matter.

It's how you love and how others love you. That's all that counts.

I was a good boy. My mother loved me and I loved her. As I died, I passed the Big Test—it's hard to make huge mistakes at sixteen.

The Coast Guard's arrival signaled that my time was not over. As the ambulance rushed to the hospital, I thought, "now that I learned the meaning of life, what will I do?"

At forty-two, I still think about this lesson each hour. I make mistakes—plenty of them—but I am guided. I chose public service, human rights, and people less fortunate for my work. At home, I make sure everyone knows how much I love them. I will face the Big Test next time after a longer life spent on what really counts: love.

Congressman Mark Kirk, 10th District, Illinois

did know everything—he knew about his dog Lucky! Then a shadow of worry crossed Ryan's face as he told me that Lucky was waiting for him to come home.

"Tell me more about Lucky," Santa said.

Ryan brightened and told me about the love of his life. Lucky was the Siberian Husky his family had gotten as a puppy after their bunny had died the summer before. Ryan and Lucky instantly became best friends and constant companions. It was Lucky who was always there to sit close and snuggle when Ryan became sick. It was Lucky's joyous greeting that included a ritual of jumping, barking, running in circles, and then licking Ryan's face when Ryan returned from his doctor and hospital visits that always broke the tension and made Ryan laugh. It was Lucky who Ryan was now worried about. Despite his own illness, Ryan didn't want his dog to be alone. He was afraid Lucky was cold or lonely. He wanted to get his surgery over with so he could go back

What I've learned about giving is that the giver is really the recipient. I hear this sentiment all the time from donors to the Elizabeth Glaser Pediatric AIDS Foundation. They say, "but it is I that should be thanking you for giving me the opportunity to offer this gift of hope." I too feel blessed that I've been given the opportunity in my lifetime to be a part of the Foundation's work. I received this gift albeit at a great price, the loss of my dearest friend Elizabeth Glaser, but I know that what Susan DeLaurentis, Elizabeth, and I gave birth to together has made an important impact on the lives of so many children around the world. That feeling is not only a gift, but also a privilege.

SUSIE ZEEGAN, COFOUNDER, THE ELIZABETH GLASER
PEDIATRIC AIDS FOUNDATION

home and give his dog all the loving he was missing out on. "When I get home," Ryan said, "I'm going to hug Lucky so hard and then I'm going to kiss her and let her lick my face all over! For Christmas, Santa, I just want to go home and be with Lucky." Ryan again laid his head in my beard and again all noise and movement stopped—not a creature was stirring, not even a mouse. We all seem to instinctively know that love is best heard in the silence.

How lucky for me, on this last day of my Christmas tour, to have had the opportunity to meet Ryan who had so much to teach me. Ryan, in his mere four years, had learned a lesson so many of us never grasp. He knew that the real treasures in life are not those of great wealth, fame, or commercial accomplishment, but rather the real treasures abound where love is. Love is the most valuable possession of all. Do you have the kind of love in your life that Ryan has? It's the kind of love that lets us see beyond ourselves. It's love that takes the focus off our own problems and shows us the needs of others. True love, like the love between a boy and his dog, is the kind that brings us out of our own misery and gives us a reason to reach out to others. This kind of love makes the magic of miracles possible because love that is unconditional and pure knows no limitations. Today is a good day to reach past your own worries and to give love to someone in need.

A CHILD IS LOST

After a good night's sleep, Santa's tour continued. We visited another hospital, prepared to greet more children with refreshed cheerfulness. Our first stop on this day was at a children's intensive care unit (ICU). Like others I had seen, this ICU was impressive and at the same time intimidating. The lights were bright and the staff was busy competently administering to their little patients who were all connected by many wires to the monitors that signaled in various tones and beeps the respiration rate, oxygen levels, and heart function. The noise of the monitoring equipment sometimes seemed to muffle the sounds of children struggling to overcome illnesses and injuries.

This unit was a particularly large room housing about 30 children and I planned to visit each one of them. I looked around for our guide and found the assigned nurse standing against the wall looking rather glum and sad-eyed. With no enthusiasm at all she stepped forward, greeted us, and then introduced Santa to a six-year-old boy named Harry. Harry was doing so well that his parents were preparing to move him from this intensive care area to a room down the hall in the regular children's wing. "Hey, Santa," said Harry, who spoke a bit hoarsely because of the tube that had been placed down his throat during his stay here, "will you be able to find me in my new room?"

"Of course, of course," Santa answered with merry laughter. "I always know where all the children are! Why don't you tell me exactly what you want for Christmas."

As Harry rattled off his list, the nurse tugged at my red coat. "Come on, Santa," she said in a forlorn tone. "There are many more children to see."

As we stepped away from Harry's bedside, I stopped short. Turning to the nurse, I asked, "Is something wrong? You seem very sad."

"I am sad, Santa," she said looking at her clipboard rather than at me. "A child from this unit died last night."

ARTWORK BY CALVIN

"Oh, I'm so sorry to hear that," I said. "That must be very painful for you. Do you want us to postpone our visit?"

She shot me a stern look and replied as she moved me toward the next bed, "We can't quit caring for these kids because one dies. There are plenty more who still need our attention — and they need to see Santa Claus."

The next child was too sick to sit up and give Santa a hug, but as I held her hand, I felt her fingers give mine a faint squeeze. This ten-year-old with short, blonde hair and beautiful, round hazel eyes and long lashes had been hit by a car while riding her bicycle on the sidewalk. Her mom told me that it was a drunk driver who got out of the car, saw the little girl bleeding on the ground, and then jumped back in his car and fled. She had a few broken bones, a concussion, and some internal bleeding but, thank God, would heal and be well enough to get back on her bike one day. "Well, sweetheart," said Santa, "I am very glad I stopped by here today so I could meet such a brave little girl. I'm going to be sure to find something very special to bring you this Christmas." As I said goodbye and noticed the broad, bright smile that lit up her face, it occurred to me that that smile was probably the only body movement she could make without great pain.

The spirit of helping others has been a driving force in my life. It is teaching, showing and bringing people together to make a difference in the lives of those less fortunate. My joys are those that come from love, passion, and compassion.

DONNA KARAN, FASHION DESIGNER

We stopped one after the other with children who all were anxious to put aside their own pain to welcome Santa. Every one of them hugged their teddy bears—some with gusto, some with tenderness. In addition, they all gave their thanks with the most precious offering of all—a child's smile.

Unfortunately, the last child on my list would have to wait to hug his bear. This two-year-old boy was recovering from open-heart surgery and was under heavy sedation to keep him still. Looking at the boy with his straight black hair lying limp against his dark skin and his eyes closed in slumber, I might have mistaken him for a healthy youngster taking an afternoon nap. But the many monitoring wires attached to the boy made it clear that this was a very sick child. He wasn't aware of his mom and dad who sat, keeping vigil by his side and he wouldn't have any memory of Santa's visit. But still his bedside was an important stop. Family members, too, need to hear some words of encouragement.

Although my initial goal was to be with the children, I found that grief-stricken relatives were also deserving of a little extra love and attention. It is hard to watch someone you love suffer each day, especially when you know there is nothing you can do to help. The only thing you can do is to be there.

"This is for your little boy," I said handing a bear to the weary young mother. "And here is another one for you. You know, you are

loved, too, for all you've been through and all you give to your child just by being here for him." These simple words of support made this mother's eyes well with tears. It was obvious that her nerves were worn thin and her emotions were on edge. "Santa knows," I continued, "that even big people sometimes need a teddy bear to hug." As I left, I saw the worried mom bury her face in the bear's soft fur and cry.

As I turned to wave goodbye to all the children, I noticed the same melancholy nurse who had accompanied us at the beginning of our visit. Her shoulders sagged with the weariness of carrying such a heavy loss. I gave her a merry "ho-ho-ho" as I often did with doctors and nurses I met on my visits and hoped for a little smile. She looked up, her eyes dark with fatigue.

"Can Santa give you a big hug this morning?" I asked.

Without another word she dropped the chart on the floor, put both arms around my neck, and wept profusely. Finally, she managed to pull herself together, wiping makeup streaks from her face.

Placing her hands gently on my shoulders, she said in a whisper, "Thanks, Santa, I needed that. The child we lost last night was my patient. I know people think that nurses get used to people dying, but every time I lose a child, it hurts."

As I drove away from the hospital, I thought more about this unhappy nurse. I thought about her willingness to love the children she cares for even at the risk of the pain it may bring. Surely she experiences more instances of child death than most people in the world will ever see—yet she still opens her heart to each child. She ignores the advice of many medical professionals to stay uninvolved emotionally. Instead, she gets up each morning and gives her heart away to frightened and ill children. I thought also how hard it must be for her even in happy cases when she is able to nurse children back to good health; she spends time getting to know them and caring for them, knowing all the time that they will soon leave.

How many of us can love so unselfishly? So often we keep people at arm's length so they can't get close enough to hurt us. We keep ourselves emotionally "safe" by staying distant and uninvolved. We don't want to get too close and risk the possibility of rejection. However, each time we turn away from someone who might bring love into our lives, we lose the potential for a wonderful relationship. Yes, people we love may not return the love, they may leave us, or they may die. But watching the kind of love this nurse has for her young patients teaches us to take the risk—to love often and deeply.

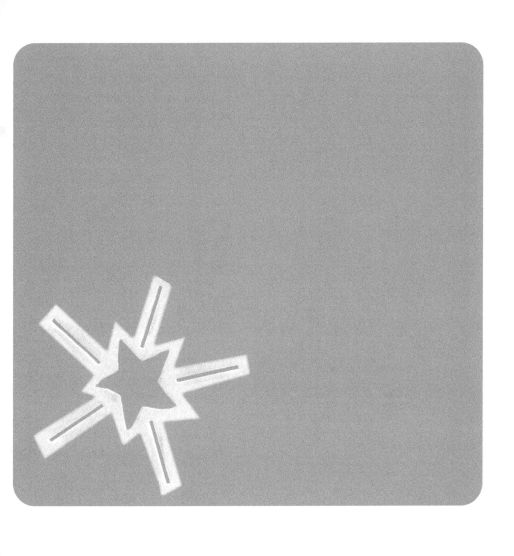

THE OUTPATIENT CLINIC

a stop for Santa in most hospitals is the outpatient clinic where people of all ages come to receive prescribed medication, routine checkups, or follow-up treatment. I found right away that the environment in a clinic is different from that of the hospital inpatient floors. Waiting rooms are filled with worried parents and commodious children. Nurses rush in and out, calling names, as doctors hurry between examination rooms. It is a crowded, boisterous place where Santa is always welcomed with squeals, laughter, and outstretched hands.

In particular, I remember one outpatient clinic in Philadelphia. I walked in and was immediately swarmed by a mob of kids, shouting and tugging at my coattails. Making my way across the lobby to the corner set up for Santa's visit, I found myself dragging at least

20 squirming and giggling children in my wake. When I finally made my way to the large Santa chair, I noticed an enormous pine tree standing nearby. The tree was laden with beautiful decorations, but not the kind that are carefully placed and organized by color and shape and size. The skilled hand of a thoughtful and artistic adult did not arrange them. No, this tree proudly wore amateur constructions of boldly colored shapes, drawings, and ornaments created by the small hands of youngsters who had visited the clinic and left their mark. The tree

breathed of childhood, of children's joys, worries, and wishes. Like Santa, a Christmas tree like this—of, for, and by children—is a symbol of love that speaks to children in a language few adults can hear or understand.

My musings on this tree were quickly cut short by the children calling anxiously for my attention. They all had so much to tell Santa. I imagined that they each had long gift lists memorized that they would whisper in my ear with high hopes for owning the mounds of toys they'd seen advertised on TV. However, I was wrong—and surprised. Again believing in the super power of the man in the red suit, most of the children asked me for gifts more precious than toys. A diabetic child wanted to be able to return to school. A boy with leukemia wanted to be well enough to play baseball again. A girl with birth defects caused by her mother's drug addiction wanted her family back together. As child after child sat on my knee, they exposed the fractures of their young lives with candor and trust. It was difficult not to wilt under the weight of their humble requests. How much simpler it would be for Santa if these children wanted a doll or a truck.

With each tug on the heart strings, I struggled to strike a balance between feel-good answers and the truth. It was a tough line to walk. I wanted to give hope, but not lies. I held each child's hand tightly and admitted that I would try hard but could not promise to deliver these kinds of gifts. Then I offered each boy and girl the gift of a teddy bear that brought back a smile for the moment.

Our teddy bears were always in high demand in those clinics. Parents often asked for more than one, for their children in tow or at home. Santa doesn't discriminate against color, gender, or ethnic background. He certainly couldn't discriminate against one's state of health, either. How could Santa give to one child, and refuse another? Needless to say, we quickly ran out of bears. A rush order was sent out to acquire more and we had to reach into our leftover stock of the previous year's teddies to make it through the visit.

Trying to ease the demand, I remember seeing a nurse pull a teenage girl out of the line saying she was too old to get a teddy bear—but time after time the girl returned to the line. She was shabbily dressed and noticeably pregnant. In my heart, I knew that this was one child who perhaps more than many others desperately needed to hug a bear offering the promise "You are loved."

When she finally reached the front of the line, the teen looked quite embarrassed and tried to hide her bulging stomach behind her

I could explain it in fancier terms but being generous toward others is, simply, the right thing to do. In fact, I am pretty sure it's why we are here.

MARY STEENBURGEN, ACTRESS

coat. "All I want is a teddy bear, Santa," she said plaintively. "Can I have a teddy bear?"

"Of course!" I bellowed with joy and handed her what I knew might be the only gift she would receive that Christmas. She gently, almost reverently, took the stuffed animal from me and, closing her eyes, she embraced it tightly.

"You are loved, you know," I told her. She opened her eyes and looked at me quizzically as if I had said something she had not considered possible. Then she smiled shyly as her eyes welled with tears. "Thank you, Santa," she said as she walked away—back to her life that held such uncertainty and pain.

I left the clinic that day physically exhausted, emotionally drained, and wearing a very rumpled Santa suit. Like a child's favorite blanket, my costume was getting love-worn. Looking down at the patches of squashed red velvet on my thighs, where hundreds of little behinds had

To me, giving is a circle formed from a mosaic of many lives, each linked to help and enhance the others. Giving, you see, is really giving back . . . and the more you give back, the more we and our world are enriched.

AMBER CHAND, COFOUNDER, EZIBA

sat, I thought of a day years ago, when our puppy ate the ear off my daughter's favorite teddy. My wife consoled her, saying, "It gives him character and more reason for you to love him." I felt like that old teddy. The more children that pulled on my coat, tugged on my beard, or sat on my lap, the more my heart opened to hold all the love they poured out to me. For the rest of my life, I will remember that day of simple and reciprocal love. That's what often happens when you put yourself in a position to give someone just a few moments of unconditional love — you get back far more than you could ever give out.

THE JOY OF TEAMWORK

*T*he typical hospital corridor is filled with doctors and nurses rushing about with their clipboards from room to room, maneuvering their way around all the medicine carts and gurneys scattered along the hallways. In the midst of this daily rush, I show up—a businessman in a Santa suit— with my entourage in tow and a wagon filled with teddy bears. I know the sounds of laughter and jingling bells throw the normally austere hospital routine askew. From my point of view, that's a good thing. For just a little while, Santa chases away the oppressive atmosphere of tension. He breaks up the boredom of little ones on the mend, confined to one room. He reminds worried parents what it feels like to smile. And in most instances, he gives a brief respite to the medical and support people as well.

One of my favorite stops on every floor is at the nurses' station. Like a heart beating lifeblood to the extremities, the stations are the

In November of 1967, a one-month "I Am Loved"® button promotion was launched. I discovered this idea while scribbling out ads as I had done since I was 10 years old. Now at age 33, I had fallen uncontrollably, insanely, and incontrovertibly in love. Unable to contain my emotions, yet embarrassed at the self-promotion of a button that said "I Am Loved,"® it immediately went in the wastebasket. Fortunately, I fished it out, took it to our highly talented advertising artist, Claude Burk, and he said he liked it. Brother Charles immediately said, "We must try it!" Dad said, "I don't like it ... it will fill our stores with hippies, but if you are going to do it, do it right!" Forty million buttons and 35 years of wedded bliss later, the button still warms hearts and in Dad's words, "Puts a smile on everyone's face!"

BARNETT C. HELZBERG, JR.,

"I AM LOVED"® IS A REGISTERED TRADEMARK OWNED BY
THE SHIRLEY AND BARNETT HELZBERG FOUNDATION.

active control centers that sustain the life of the unit. I have tremendous respect for the nurses I have met over the years; they possess a wellspring of strength that sustains them in this environment of pain and sadness. Because they are so devoted to their work, my sudden appearance is often seen as a disruption. When I first intrude on their hectic day, I get a few half-hearted smiles from nurses busy on the phone, or talking with parents, or recording vital information on their charts. Sometimes, I even get a warning look that clearly says, "Can't you see I'm too busy to play games?" I have the highest respect for their work but I also know that if I persist it will take only a few moments to get most of them laughing and hamming it up for the camera. To break the ice, I've developed a comic routine in which I tease the nurses as I pretend to flip through patient charts, sit in their chairs, and call Mrs. Claus from their phones. Then we gather round

for a group shot of Santa with all the nurses, arms slung over each other's shoulders and smiling with joy. That's when I try to make a break and get back to my rounds of the children's rooms, but it never fails that the nurses begin to beg for a personal picture with Santa. "Oh, Santa," they often say, "my kids would just love to see a picture of me with you. Would you mind?" Others are a little more demanding. I remember one especially sturdy nurse saying, "You're not going anywhere big man until I get my picture taken with you!" as she hugged my shoulder and mugged for the camera.

I have found it a bit more difficult to get the doctors to warm up to the idea of a Santa on the floor. They tend to acknowledge me with a sense of reservation that, at times, borders on annoyance, especially when they see Santa Claus prowling about the halls, disrupting the system. One day I approached a physician on his rounds.

"Hi, Doc," I said. "How's your day?"

"Okay," he replied, seemingly disconcerted by my intrusion.

"Well," I said as cheerfully as possible, "I hope you have a very Merry Christmas."

I waved goodbye as he stalked off down the hall muttering to himself. I hoped that, despite his demeanor, I might have planted a small seed of encouragement.

While I often fail to get physicians excited about a Santa visit, I know I can count on the many members of the support staff to make me feel welcome. I remember meeting an elderly lady who wore a housekeeping nametag on her green uniform. She was a stately woman in her mid-sixties, with snow-white hair, pushing a cart that

Perhaps the best gift my parents ever gave me was my annual adventure as a camper at Camp Keewaydin in rural Vermont. Not a day goes by that I don't draw from the lessons I learned under the northern New England skies.

As an adult, it has provided me particular joy to give the gift that my parents once gave me. First, I did this by sending my own children to Keewaydin, and, when they returned, I relished hearing their stories and seeing their growth. Fortunately, I was able to find a way to continue giving this gift after my sons had grown—by funding scholarships for other children to attend Keewaydin. Indeed, one of the many virtues of the rough-hewn camp life is that it is the great leveler: once kids get off the bus, they're all just campers.

In funding these scholarships, I'm not really the one giving the gift. The dedicated people who operate Keewaydin are the ones doing the giving. I'm just thrilled to be able to help them give their life-altering gift to a new generation.

MICHAEL D. EISNER, CHAIRMAN AND CEO,
HAS BEEN WITH THE WALT DISNEY COMPANY SINCE 1984.

held a bucket and mop. She watched me with curious eyes as I walked over to her.

"Merry Christmas," I said with a smile.

"Thank you, Santa," she said, beaming back at me. "I've been watching you with the kids and I wonder, could you do me a favor?"

"What's that?" I asked.

"Can you give me a great big hug?"

"It would be a privilege," I replied.

So there, in the middle of the hallway, Santa Claus and an old woman in a custodial uniform embraced, mop and all.

"Thank you," she said with great dignity. (I learned later that this little lady was the pride and joy of the unit. Everyone loved her and was pleased to see her get some special attention from Santa Claus.)

Around lunchtime on that day, I decided to grab a bite to eat. I was anxious for the haven of the staff cafeteria where, in the safety of an all-adult environment, I could remove my beard and wig. No matter how hot it gets, I can't let the kids see me out of costume. Seeing

Santa Claus with beard in hand would shatter their faith and trust in the jolly old man.

I finished eating and got up to leave, when I felt a tap on my shoulder. It was the same doctor I'd spoken to earlier that morning— only this time his dour frown was replaced with a hint of a smile.

"You're okay, Santa," he told me. "You really cheered up some of my young patients this morning and that's good medicine. I guess we make a decent team. Keep up the good work."

ARTWORK BY MITCHELL

That was the first time I realized that Santa truly is part of a team. While doctors work with medical facts, and nurses take care of back-up support and paperwork, and support staff looks after mopping and cleaning, Santa is in charge of tempering all of this work with unconditional love.

He adds something important to the mix that no one else can. Yes, Santa is a team player.

This experience of being part of a team has taught me a valuable lesson. In my own life, I have often asked the question, "I'm just one person, what difference can I make?" Now I know. Alone, it is difficult to make this world a better place. What kind of hospital would it be if doctors alone worked there—no nurses, no social services, no custodial staff? Or, what if only social service people worked there? Or only custodial staff? None of them can be effective alone. They all need each other. We all need one another to make a difference in the world. By adding my small contribution to the work of hundreds of others, things are done, the lives of others improve, and as a bonus, my own life is enriched.

If you're ever tempted to underestimate the power of your contribution to others and to society, remember that you are not in this alone. Think of yourself as a simple, singular raindrop. Alone, your life might easily go unnoticed and without purpose. But working along with others who have the same goal, the force of your combined power can literally move mountains—or in the very least, comfort the sick, feed the hungry, clothe the poor, and shelter the homeless.

Reflection by
BILL BELFIORE

Bill Belfiore is the senior managing director of corporate bonds at Fimat USA, Inc. (a division of Société Générale). He is an accomplished business-man who never imagined that one day he would be making headlines for adopting four HIV-positive children from Romania. But as Bill has discov-ered, life has a way of leading you to unexpected sources of love if you are open to the opportunity.

In the fall of 1989, my wife Susan and I were watching a *Primetime* special hosted by Diane Sawyer about children in Romania living in orphanages; they were all HIV-positive after receiving tainted transfusions. At the end of the show, Brother Toby McCarroll from Starcross Community invited viewers to join his program and go to Romania as a volunteer for six months to nurture these children with love and affection. At that point, Susan and I had been married 20 years and had no children of our own. We both turned from the TV and looked at each other and, although looking back I don't know why or how, we both knew this was right for us.

Susan temporarily closed her body works practice in New Jersey and left for Romania in January 1990. She was assigned to five babies between the ages of one and two. She was given a two-room area where they all lived together. During my first visit, I saw that although none of the children had any illnesses or symptoms of HIV, they were in great need. They lived in steel cribs; they had no diapers or hot water; the food was unappealing and, although the people who worked there were doing the best they could, the environment was really abominable.

But in the midst of this deprivation, I was absolutely amazed by the power of love that I witnessed. Life got instantly better the moment my wife walked into the lives of these children. She couldn't change their environment, but they were so happy to have her love. Everything else didn't matter to them.

They never felt sorry for themselves and they didn't complain; they were just so happy to have a mother who would love them. At the same time, although my wife was living in very difficult conditions, I had never seen her so happy. It wasn't long before both of us were deeply in love with these children.

After my first visit, I remember thinking as I left, "I wonder what life will be like for us when this six months is over?" It wasn't long before I knew that our lives would never be the same when I got an excited phone call from my wife. "What do you think," she asked, "about adopting one of these children?" Without even thinking, I heard myself saying, "Why don't we adopt all of them?" I guess this came right out of my heart because I sure didn't think about what I was saying (although I haven't regretted it one day since). Susan laughed and admitted that she had planned to work up to that idea! Since then my wife has said, "Your heart allows you to go places where your head wouldn't," and boy is she right. Not thinking about any of the consequences, we jumped into what turned out to be a very long and difficult adoption process. We loved these children and that's all that really mattered to us. We didn't stop and analyze their health situation. We didn't calculate how long they might live or the medical care they would need. We needed them as much as they needed us and we just kept working toward the goal of bringing them home.

My wife spent the next two years living with the children while battling the Romanian authorities. Government officials were very suspicious of our motives and gave Susan an incredibly hard time. There were many times when their stonewalling tactics made us think that this just wasn't going to happen. But we knew we couldn't give up because of the bonds we'd made with these children. I think my wife just literally wore the authorities down. After two years, she finally got the adoption papers signed, quickly packed the children up, and left for Bucharest. Worried that they might change their minds (again), she was ready to take the first plane out of there no matter where it was going!

I didn't hear about this until she got to Frankfurt. She called me and said she'd be home in the morning with our four new children. (One of the original five was returned to his parents when retesting found him not to be HIV-positive.) I hung up and broke out in a cold sweat. "What have I just done?" I thought. However, it was too late now to start thinking with my head. The next day my wife arrived home with our four-year-old Ramona and three three-year-olds: Ionel, Mihaela, and Loredana. (As another happy surprise, three years later after twenty-four years of marriage at the age of forty-five, God blessed us once again when my wife gave birth to our son Aidan. I've certainly learned never say never.)

In these past ten years, I have seen the concrete power of love. I've recently learned that most of the thirty children who were in the orphanage with my children have since died. These children were in bad shape. Our Loredana was only eight pounds at two years old. Now my children are in their teens and are very healthy. I know they have the benefit of good medical care, but I'll never underplay the role of love—not only in how it has improved their lives, but also in how their love has improved mine. It's hard to explain it without using a bunch of clichés about love, but these children really have given me a much deeper understanding of what love is. Before they came into my life, I know I loved my wife and my parents, but this love is so much more; my whole life now has much deeper meaning because of them. Being open to all the opportunities to reach out to those around us gives all of us the chance to find love in places we never would have suspected.

PART V

A Call *to*
ACTION

A CALL TO ACTION

*W*e Americans are a generous lot. We give away more of our time and our money than any other nation. As individuals, we gave nearly $200 billion in the year 2000 to charities critical to health and human services, education, religion, international affairs, the arts and humanities, and protecting the environment. We are a nation that has produced fabulously wealthy families—Carnegie, Ford, Rockefeller—whose gifts have brought libraries, hospitals, and universities to life. These

89 percent of households give to charity.
Source: Independent Sector

early philanthropists led the way for the millions of Americans who today donate their money and volunteer their time in local schools, churches, mosques, and synagogues. In fact, the beginning of the twenty-first century has been called an era of new wealth and new social consciousness; it has been dubbed "a golden age of philanthropy in America."

My call tonight is for every American to commit at least two years, four thousand hours over the rest of your lifetime, to the service of your neighbors and your nation.

PRESIDENT GEORGE W. BUSH,

THE STATE OF THE UNION, JANUARY 29, 2002

Our image as the strongest and most generous nation on the planet was tested when the unthinkable happened on September 11, 2001. In the aftermath of the terrorist attacks, millions of Americans passed

> 70 percent of Americans participated in some form of charity following September 11.
> *Source:* Independent Sector/Wirthlin Worldwide

that horrific test when they rallied as a united nation. While we mourned the loss of innocent lives and the loss of heroic rescue workers, we flew our American flags and we cheered our military. And then we gave. Millions of donors gave nearly $1.3 billion through February of 2002 to the American Red Cross Liberty Fund, the September 11 Fund, and the Salvation Army. We gave so much blood

> 73 percent of those who gave to September 11 funds say they will continue to give to other charities.
> *Source:* Independent Sector/Wirthlin Worldwide

that the Red Cross was overwhelmed. We donated water, food, dry socks, gloves, and face masks that piled high in volunteer comfort stations around Ground Zero. And we bought baked goods and hand-made flag pins from schoolchildren determined to do their part.

The American Red Cross received nearly 1.2 million units of blood between September 11 and October 30—compared to 380,000 units expected during that timeframe.
Source: American Red Cross

Now, as we move beyond the tragedies of September 11, we can take the spirit and the strength gained from that experience and use it to give more. There is still much more work to be done to battle the everyday tragedies that still surround us such as poverty, illiteracy, and homelessness. In addition, there are great personal rewards yet to be gained because our gifts will mean so much to so many.

This chapter explores the many reasons we *should* give and the many ways we *can* give. It also provides specific information on

"I received a charity solicitation the other day," commented a young man to several of his friends gathered to watch a sporting event. "You never give to charity," they teased. "I gave in my office the day after September 11," he protested. "Isn't every day a day after September 11?"

charities and organizations that make it easy to give your wealth, time, and talent.

GIVING YOUR TREASURE

We live in a great country. Historically, America has had a caring and compassionate heart for children, families, and individuals who are less fortunate and in need of help. Today, this compassion is validated by facts: Individuals donate nearly $100 billion annually to charities and groups that provide health and human services, education, arts and culture, or promote a healthy environment. We donate another $100 billion to religious organizations. That's $200 billion every year!

As government's role in promoting societal care has declined, the need for these private funds to invigorate communities has increased. Today, foundations, corporations, associations, and individuals fund many of this country's hospitals, universities, religious organizations, cultural

> $203.45 billion was given to charity by private individuals in 2000 —
> 83 percent of gifts were from individuals.
> *Source:* Giving USA/AAFRC Trust for Philanthropy

institutions, museums, local schools, and health care clinics. While foundations and corporations make up $35 billion of overall giving, it's individuals who give an astonishing 75 percent of all the funding that charities receive. Yes, that is a great deal of money. But we are a big country and, unfortunately, that money is simply not enough to reach all those in need.

The average American gives only about 3.2 percent of his or her income to charity. (Surprisingly, the people who give the most actually

The average household donates $1,620 per year or just $3 per day.
Source: Independent Sector

make the least. Households below the poverty line — $10,000 a year — give 5.2 percent of their income to charity.) If we each began to give our fair share starting today, what an impact we could have!

There are 11.6 million poor children in the United States.
One in six children (16.2 percent) grows up in poverty.
Source: Children's Defense Fund

That fair share could be achieved through just a small increase in giving. Instead of giving $30 to help disabled children, what if we gave $33?

Calculate your gift:

Your Income		*Average donated*		*Your Gift*
$_____	×	3.2 percent	=	$_____

Instead of giving $100 to a shelter for homeless families, what if we gave $110? If every American increased his or her giving by just a few dollars, it could mean an extra $10 billion each year to help children, the elderly, the sick, the poor, and those who may have lost hope for a better life.

> In 2001, nearly 23 million Americans sought food assistance.
> *Source:* America's Second Harvest

Look at the amount of money you gave to charity last year and increase it, slightly, this year. The extra money that you alone give may seem small but, combined with the gifts of others, together we can affect true change and support quality-of-life improvements in our global community.

> For every 1 percent increase in giving, an additional $2 billion is generated for charities and religious organizations.

GIVING YOUR TIME AND TALENT

We are all neighbors. Especially after September 11, we learned how much we care about and support one another. We learned how good it feels to help others in need. We learned that when we share ourselves, even with strangers, we automatically become better human beings. To keep and own the good feeling that comes from being

83.9 million adults volunteered nearly 15.5 billion hours in 2000.
Source: Independent Sector

useful and generous, we need to stay involved in the lives of others. We need to continually give the ultimate charitable gift — our time and our talent.

Just as we have been a generous nation with our treasure, we have been equally generous with our time and talent. Nearly 44 percent of adults volunteer and nearly 70 percent of those volunteers do so

44 percent of adults volunteer.
Source: Independent Sector

monthly or more often. Those who volunteer regularly, donate nearly 24 hours per month to the organizations they assist. But like financial

> In the United States, 109 million volunteers do $255 billion worth of charitable work every year.
> *Source:* Promo Magazine 2/2000

donations, the number of volunteers in this country does not begin to meet the needs of the nonprofit and religious organizations that rely so heavily on the goodwill of others. You are needed.

As you start to think about how you can best help others, you may wonder what motivates people to volunteer. Well, the reasons for sharing time with others less fortunate are personal and unique to each person's situation. Some people offer a piece of themselves in order to share their own good fortune. After their children are grown, some fill the empty nest with good deeds. Some people are called to action when disease strikes a family member. Others become involved in social activism when complacency threatens their values or way of life. There are as many reasons to help as there are people in need of that help.

> 28 percent of Americans volunteer with family members.
> *Source:* Independent Sector

Sometimes a life-altering incident unexpectedly catapults people into situations where their own personal struggles help others along a path of rehabilitation. Pamela's story retells her journey from recovery to philanthropy:

> *Pamela is not your typical donor of time and talent. Though she had been a volunteer most of her life—doing a stint with the Peace Corps right out of college, donating part of her time as a psychotherapist to working pro bono with at-risk youth—her work with the Northern Virginia Brain Injury Association came as much as a surprise to her as it came as a gift to the members of her support group.*
>
> *Leaving her apartment one morning, Pamela was struck on the head by a falling window with enough force to cause brain injury. Trapped by depression, confusion, and other symptoms associated with brain injury, Pamela lost her practice and her patients, as her life spiraled into disorder. After trying therapies and treatments that never seemed to help, Pamela found support with the Northern Virginia Brain Injury Association.*

The support group was a welcome relief. Pamela met others who shared her problems. It soon became evident that the support group could use a skilled facilitator. Pamela became not just a participant in the group, but a facilitator using her skills as a therapist. She was elected the group's president and 10 years later, Pamela still gives her time and talent each year as emcee and facilitator of the organization's annual conference.

Mentoring Resources

National Mentoring Partnership
888-432-6368
www.mentoring.org

Big Brothers Big Sisters of America
215-567-7000
www.bbbsa.org

Mentoring USA
212-253-1194 ext. 459
www.mentoringUSA.org

GIVING IN KIND

Giving in kind—even the term sounds friendly. And friendly it is. In-kind giving, sometimes also called product philanthropy, has become a major form of corporate charity. In-kind gifts can be just about anything, such as clothing, food and water, medical supplies, office supplies, educational materials, recreational equipment, consumer products, technology, and office equipment. IBM Corp., for example, has created a nationwide technology donation program in which it donates equipment to charitable agencies that provide early learning programs, youth education services, family and adult services such as literacy and job training.

Charitable agencies need these in-kind donations to survive. In 2000, the value of product donations to Gifts In Kind International (the world's leading charity in product philanthropy) totaled $455 million, increasing by nearly a third over the previous year.

This generous in-kind giving has allowed Gifts In Kind to distribute nearly $2.5 billion since 1983 in product donations to the world's leading charities.

> Gifts in Kind International is the world's
> leading charity in product philanthropy.
> *www.giftsinkind.com*

Product Donations Are Up

According to *The Chronicle of Philanthropy*, product donations by the top 150 companies in the United States made up more than 30 percent of total 1999 contributions. These companies reported charitable giving totaling $2.5 billion in cash and $1.1 billion in products during 1999.

Giving in kind is a win-win charitable plan for both the companies that give and nonprofits who receive. Companies can benefit from tax deductions while at the same time reducing the cost of carrying excess inventories. These companies may also enjoy good public relations and recognition for their donations. At the same time, product donations not only allow non-profits to fulfill their mission, they also provide financial savings and increased efficiencies through donated equipment and software.

Does your company produce goods or equipment? If so, what does it do with over stock or outdated equipment? Ask your company to consider product philanthropy today.

RAISING A GIVING SOCIETY

Can you remember the first time you gave time or money to a charitable cause? Many adults who first experienced philanthropy as a child say it filled them with a sense of accomplishment. It made them feel useful and grown-up. Researchers who study the development of the "volunteer personality" say that those who have early experiences with charitable acts often continue the habit in adulthood. For this reason, it's vital that we give our children the opportunity to enjoy the gifts of giving.

> *Chuck Bolte, now the executive director of a well-known children's charity, was sure (even two decades ago, long before he had this job) that he wanted his children to learn about philanthropy and charitable giving from the youngest possible age. When each of his children became old enough to receive a weekly allowance, Chuck made boxes for them, divided into four sections. Into the first three sections, each child was instructed to place a portion of his or her allowance for clothing,*

a portion for snacks and food, and a portion for fun. The children were actively encouraged to use some of their money for entertainment, even as they learned responsibility for life's necessities. After all, there are many facets of life. Into the fourth chamber of the box, the children were to place 10 percent of their allowance, to be given away to a worthy cause. It didn't matter to whom they gave their 10 percent—the church, a charity, a good cause. What mattered was that they gave. And they did. All of Chuck's children took that simple lesson to heart and today continue to support a variety of national and local charitable organizations.

Lessons like these teach children early in life that social responsibility is a part of daily living. They also set the foundation for tempering the me-first teen years. While the word *teen* doesn't usually conjure up images of charity, giving, and caring, the fact is that 59 percent of

> 59 percent of teenagers volunteer an average of 3.5 hours per week, totaling 2.4 billion hours of volunteer time annually.
> *Source:* Independent Sector

teenagers volunteer their time an average of three-and-half hours a week. In suburban New Jersey at Hawthorne High School, community service by teenagers is alive and well through a program called SHARE. In 1985 teacher Patti Atkinson-Battista organized six teens into a group called Students of Hawthorne Acting Responsibly and Effectively — SHARE for short. Today the group boasts a membership of over one-third of the student body. These teenagers are involved in many community service activities that spark their interest in volunteering, but their all-time favorite, on-going programs are those that give them opportunities to make young, inner-city kids laugh and in return learn themselves what real joy feels like.

These eight- and nine-year-old kids have seen more awful things and have been through more than I have at age eighteen, and yet they still get up every morning and have this hunger for life. This inspired me. I know I have so much and I also know that I forget to be thankful for it. I think of those kids in the Bronx and I remember that life doesn't have to be about material things; it's about living the life you have to the fullest. Because I got to spend time with them, I know I'll always look at life a little differently. These kinds of experiences are empowering. I know I can't change the world by myself, but now because of some really great kids in the Bronx I do feel that I'm capable of having a profound effect on it.

CHRIS CIVITARESE, HAWTHORNE HIGH SCHOOL, NEW JERSEY

After the teen years, it's easy to cast aside charitable acts in the hectic young-adult world where college, marriage, and new careers sap energy and time. However, based on the actions of the so-called Generation X and Generation Y young adults, the future of philanthropy is in good hands. These are the young people we sent off to colleges and universities at historic rates. This is the group who has developed an admirable tolerance for differences in culture and beliefs and has marked their world with an innate sense of justice and fairness. They are the bright, young, caring individuals who have shown us that even when time is tight, there is a way to share it with others.

Joel Goldman retells a personal story from his college days that not only changed the course of his life, but has since exposed hundreds of thousands of university students to social action:

> I was diagnosed in 1992 before the "cocktail" medications, which now sustain so many of us living with HIV, were available. The doctor initially gave me only three to five years to live. After many sleepless nights, I made a decision to leave this earth with my character defined by social action and consciousness. With the help of a friend, I created "Friendship in the Age of AIDS," a program designed to educate college students

about the dangers of mixing sex and alcohol. That was the way I contracted HIV and I wanted to do everything I could to make sure other college students didn't make the same mistake.

1,600: The number of children worldwide infected with HIV each day.
Source: Elizabeth Glaser Pediatric AIDS Foundation

In the first seven years, we spoke at over 600 schools, reaching nearly a half million students. After hearing my story, their first question was always, "What can I do to help?"

Three years ago I contacted the Elizabeth Glaser Pediatric AIDS Foundation with an idea called Caring for Kids 101. The Foundation recognized the great potential that lay within this untapped segment of society, and to date college students working with this program have raised more than $1 million to fight pediatric AIDS. But more importantly, Caring for Kids

The memories I have of bringing kids joy makes me feel really good and it's something I want to feel again. It's kind of a selfish thing, but doing good just feels good.

JOHN HANNAH, HAWTHORNE HIGH SCHOOL, NEW JERSEY

*101 has exposed our nation's youth to service, giving, and ways
to fight against a social injustice like pediatric AIDS. And just
as I learned more than a decade ago, once you are exposed to
helping others you can never forget.*

GETTING STARTED

Did the events of September 11, 2001 change us for a few days or for a
lifetime? Have our values and life priorities really changed? Are we
now willing to do more to help people in need? The answers to these
questions depend on how you respond to the call to action. It's time
for all of us to look in our communities and workplaces for opportunities to reach out and in return gain the gift of giving. You need to
make the time in your life to find your own red hat and wear it with
conviction and pride.

Give in Your Community

In 1883, French historian Alexis de Tocqueville wrote: "These Americans
are the most peculiar people in the world ... In a local community, in
their country a citizen may conceive of some need, which is not being
met. What does he do? He goes across the street and discusses it with

his neighbor. Then what happens? A committee comes into existence and then the committee begins functioning on behalf of the need ... All of this is done by private citizens on their own initiative."

Yes, Americans have a long history of community-based philanthropy that is individually initiated. Still today, individuals or small groups with similar interests become inspired by a need they uncover within their local community or the world community. It is this kind of inspiration that gives life to programs like Helzberg Diamond's Santa's Gift. Yet, as I learned from my own experience, it's often easy to see the need; it's a bit more difficult to do something about it. The first step toward finding that need and taking action may be the hardest, but I now know that each step after leads to great rewards.

As you begin your venture into community-based philanthropy, look over the "Try It Today" list of simple ideas to get you going. Then let your heart and imagination lead the way.

Give in the Workplace

Workplace giving is a major point of access for most nonprofit organizations. The results of thousands of business-charity partnerships have been astounding. Businesses and environmental activists have joined forces to find solutions to the impact pollution has had on our environment. Large corporations have supported foreign aid organizations who bring relief and development around the globe to people struggling against challenges like war and natural disasters. Business contributions, fund raisers, and awareness programs have contributed to the mission of charity-based organizations focused on health issues ranging from breast cancer to kidney disease, heart disease, HIV/AIDS, and juvenile diabetes. Many large and small businesses participate in human service programs that address our diverse population's need for services like mentoring, hunger relief, abuse prevention programs, and educational aid in the form of scholarship programs, literacy volunteers, and programs to recruit and train teachers in America.

> *General Electric's Elfun Society is a "global organization of GE volunteers," with a membership base of over 45,000 in 118 chapters throughout the world. Elfun chapters have painted shelters in Amsterdam, cared for sick children in Shanghai, established a library in Jakarta, collected coats for Chicago school children and even found time to play Santa for hospitalized children around the world. In their 2000-2001 year, the Elfuns did more than 1,000 volunteer projects. To learn more about this workplace organization visit www.elfun.org.*

Try It Today!

- Why not forego purchasing a new CD or three cups of Starbuck's coffee this week and use the money instead to buy new books for inner-city kids?

- On your way home from the office today, stop by the supermarket, buy the makings of a good meal and donate the food to your local food pantry.

- Locate the nearest soup kitchen and offer your time once a month.

- Clean out your closet and donate your no-longer-used business attire to a charity that helps people entering the job market.

- Clear off your bookshelves and give your gently read books to the library or local schools.

- Instead of going to the movies this weekend, use that time to shoot baskets or play board games with some disadvantaged kids at an inner city YMCA.

- Offer to tutor. According to a 1992 survey by the U.S. Department of Education, there are 40 million Americans who read only at a first grade level—some can't read basic signs or complete simple forms. You can help these people.

- Become a mentor. Statistics indicate that nearly 500,000 children run away from home each year in the United States. These young people need someone to guide them and to help them with their legal and family struggles.

- If you have an interest in helping kids, contact The Heart of America Foundation. This organization was created to teach the values at the heart of America and to help people—particularly the young—learn that they help themselves when the help others. The Heart of America's activities embrace the two most time-honored forms of education: teaching by example and learning by doing. In the last five years, the program has had an impact on tens of thousands of elementary, middle, and high school students. One high-profile effort known as the Books from the Heart program addressed the enormous need children living in poverty have for books. To find out more about the Heart of America Foundation visit www.heartofamerica.org or call 202-546-3256.

- If the stories of Santa's visits with hospitalized kids moved you to don a red suit in your own community, information on how to start a Santa's Gift program can be found at www.helzberg.com.

If your place of business is involved in philanthropic activities, sign up today to help out! If your company has not yet become involved in charitable activities, give them a push to get started. You can do it alone, or reach out for help. There are several agencies designed to bring workplace donors and volunteers together with charitable organizations that need support. America's Charities is one such group.

> America's Charities is a federation of the best-known and most-loved charities in the world today, including Make-A-Wish Foundation of America, Habitat for Humanity International, Ronald McDonald House Charities, Shriners Hospitals for Children, NAACP, Amnesty International, and nearly one hundred other nonprofit organizations. America's Charities brings these organizations to employee charitable giving campaigns in workplaces all across the nation. The founding principle of America's Charities is that it is the donors' right to direct exactly where his or her contributions go—even if their charity of choice is not a member of America's Charities network. For information on America's Charities, visit www.charities.org or call 703-222-3861.

FINDING A CHARITY
THAT'S RIGHT FOR YOU

There is no shortage of people and agencies who need your help.
But you do need to know how to find them. You might begin your
search at a local place of religious worship. They are by nature
involved in charity and volunteerism. For a broader look at the possibilities, turn on your computer (or use the one at your local library).
The Internet has become both a vehicle for giving to charitable
organizations as well as for researching volunteer opportunities. The
Internal Revenue Service recognizes 819,000 charities, with 45,000
new charities added in the past year—so surely there's something out
there for you!

To encourage continued giving and volunteerism in the wake of
the September 11 tragedies, national programs like America's Caring
Heart Campaign, were developed to provide a rallying point and
practical information on how philanthropic giving by individuals can
have an immediate impact on quality of life issues for millions of
needy Americans.

To begin your search, log on at:

workingforchange.com	giveforchange.com
shopforchange.com	networkforgood.org
igive.com	charitywave.com
independentsector.org	givingday.org
volunteermatch.org	charityamerica.com
helping.org	planetsave.com
usafreedomcorps.gov	

Once you have identified a charity that interests you, check it out at www.nationalcharitiesinformationbureau.org.

America's Caring Heart Campaign is a national campaign focused on urging Americans to raise the level of their support for charities throughout the country. In the immediate aftermath of September 11, millions of Americans found great satisfaction in giving their time and money to a cause that rallied us *as a nation like no other in recent years. The campaign seeks to keep America's caring heart strong by doing just a little more to help one another in this great American family. Taken together, a "little more" by each of us will mean so much in improving the quality of life for millions of children, the elderly, the sick, and the poor. For information about America's Caring Heart Campaign, visit www.americacaringheart.com.*

AN AMERICAN TALE

The story of giving is America's story. From the beginning, we were drawn together for a common purpose—a new nation filled with individuals who pledged their life, liberty, and fortunes to build a new land. From community-led barn raisings to celebrations of the harvest and sharing the bounty, from the first Thanksgiving to September 11, 2001, this nation's unique generosity and humanity is something to be proud of.

It is our willingness to answer the call to action that has provided ongoing philanthropic support for educational services, housing needs, health and human services, and arts and culture. Without the generosity of millions of individuals, many of these services would not be available at the levels to which Americans have become accustomed. Hospitals and medical research, universities and public and private elementary and secondary schools, housing for the disadvantaged, support for visual and performing arts, and protection of the environment all depend to varying degrees on philanthropic gifts.

The American tale is one of generosity, humanity, freedom, justice, equality, and compassion. To enhance and nourish this tale, build better communities and a better world, we must continue to give. This is your call to action. Today you must decide if you will answer that call.

Through the gathering momentum of millions of acts of service and decency and kindness, I know: We can overcome evil with greater good.

PRESIDENT GEORGE W. BUSH,
THE STATE OF THE UNION, JANUARY 29, 2002

It's What in the World You Can Do!

You might be thinking, "The little bit that I can do will never help much!" or "What in the world can I do?" If you've ever spent ten minutes reading a book to a lonely child, you know that even that small amount of compassion and attention can make a world of difference. No one person can solve the world's problems, but what little you do can make your little corner of the world—or one far away from yours—a happier, healthier, safer place to live for those who need your help. Each of us can right a wrong, fill a plate, visit a shut-in, or clean up a park—and that does make a difference for us all!

Source: Networkforgood.org

EPILOGUE

Now that you've met some of Santa's kids, and maybe even had to dry a tear in the process, isn't it time to find your own "red hat?" Remember, it's only through the power of giving that we find true meaning in life.

As Jonathan said to Santa many years ago . . . "Now go and give."

JEFF
A/K/A SANTA

RESOURCE LIST OF NONPROFIT ORGANIZATIONS

America's Charities
(703)222-3861
www.charities.org

A federation of the world's best-known and most-loved charities.
The founding principle of America's Charities it that it is the donor's
right to direct exactly where his or her contributions go — even if
the charity of choice is not a member of the America's Charities
network.

America's Second Harvest
(800)771-2303
www.secondharvest.org

This is the nation's largest domestic hunger relief organization, providing food and groceries to 26 million hungry Americans each year. Their goal is to end hunger in America.

American Campaign for Prevention of Child Abuse
and Family Violence
(202)429-6695
www.americancampaign.org

Your generous financial support enables the National Council to assist thousands of abused and vulnerable children, spouses, and partners (women and men), and the elderly.

American Cancer Society
(800)227-2345
www.cancer.org

This is the largest funder of nongovernmental cancer research resulting in 30 Nobel Prize winners and breakthrough discoveries. The Society provides community-based, early detection/prevention programs and patient assistance.

American Oceans Campaign
(800)862-3260
www.americanoceans.org

The American Oceans Campaign (AOC) is a national, nonprofit organization dedicated to safeguarding the vitality of the nation's oceans and coastal waters. Founded in 1987 by actor-activist Ted Danson, AOC has offices in Washington, D.C. and Los Angeles, California.

American Red Cross
(800)435-7669
www.redcross.org

The American Red Cross is a humanitarian organization, led by volunteers, to provide relief to victims of disasters and help prevent, prepare, and respond to emergencies.

Big Brothers Big Sisters of America
(215)567-7000
www.bbbsi.org

The mission of Big Brothers Big Sisters of America is to make a positive difference in the lives of children and youth, primarily through a professionally supported one-to-one relationship with a caring adult. By providing committed volunteers, national leadership, and standards of excellence, this organization assists children in achieving their highest potential as they grow to become confident, competent, and caring individuals.

Covenant House
(800)388-3888
www.covenanthouse.org

This organization offers food, clothing, shelter, medical care, and vocational training to homeless, at-risk youth in 21 North and Central American cities. Call NINELINE (800)999-9999 for nationwide assistance.

Cure Autism Now Foundation
(888)8AUTISM
www.cureautismnow.org

Founded by parents, clinicians, and leading scientists, this foundation is dedicated to biomedical research that advances early detection, prevention, treatments, and a cure for Autism and related disorders.

Diabetes Research and Wellness Foundation
(877)633-3976
www.diabeteswellness.net

This foundation funds scientific research into treatments and cure for diabetes. It also conducts screenings and education programs to save lives from blindness, kidney failure, or amputations; it also publishes "The Diabetes Wellness Letter."

Dress for Success Worldwide
(212)532-1922
www.dressforsuccess.org

Provides business clothing appropriate for interviews to low-income women seeking employment. Women are referred by homeless shelters, domestic violence shelters, job training programs, and substance abuse programs.

The Elizabeth Glaser Pediatric AIDS Foundation
(888)499-4673
www.pedaids.org

This foundation strives to create hope for children with HIV/AIDS and other serious and life-threatening diseases. It is the only national foundation identifying, funding, and conducting pediatric AIDS research.

The Elton John AIDS Foundation
(310)535-1775
www.ejaf.org

This foundation provides funding for educational programs targeted at HIV/AIDS prevention and/or the elimination of prejudice and discrimination against HIV/AIDS-affected individuals, and for programs that provide services to people living with or at risk for HIV/AIDS.

Habitat for Humanity International
(800)422-4828
www.habitat.org

Habitat for Humanity is a Christian housing ministry working to end poverty housing by partnering with families in need to build affordable homes. It has built more than 100,000 homes worldwide.

Heart of America Foundation
(202)546-3256
www.heartofamerica.org

This foundation teaches the values at the heart of America. It also helps kids earn money for higher education by volunteering in their communities—helping themselves by helping others.

The Hole in The Wall Gang Fund
(203)772-0522
www.holeinthewallgang.org

Founded by Paul Newman, this is a nonprofit camp and year-round center, providing free services to children and their families coping with cancer and serious blood disorders.

The Humane Society of the United States
(202)452-1100
www.hsus.org

The primary and motivating mission of this society is the elimination of suffering and the prevention of cruelty to all living creatures.

Junior Achievement
(719)540-8000
www.ja.org

Join in Junior Achievement's Military Role Model Program helping students K-12 learn about business, economics, success skills, problem-solving, and critical thinking skills.

Make-A-Wish Foundation of America
(800)722-9474
www.wish.org

The Make-A-Wish Foundation grants the wishes of children with life-threatening illnesses to enrich the human experience with hope, strength, and joy.

Mothers Against Drunk Driving
(800)438-6233
www.madd.org

Mothers Against Drunk Driving provides local programs that assist victims of alcohol-related crashes and educates the public about the dangers of drunk and drugged driving and underage drinking.

National Center for Missing and Exploited Children
(888)246-2632
www.missingkids.com

The organization spearheads national and international efforts to locate and recover missing children and raises public awareness about ways to prevent child abduction, molestation, and sexual exploitation.

The Make-A-Wish Foundation is all about hope, strength, and joy—the children and families we are privileged to serve teach us by example that no challenge is too great, no dream too extreme. Our donors and volunteers fuel the dazzling fire of commitment as they express their generosity of spirit. Those who've joined our circle of compassion surround and sustain us all as we strive to fulfill our mission.

PAULA VAN NESS, PRESIDENT AND CEO,
MAKE-A-WISH FOUNDATION OF AMERICA

The Nature Conservancy
(703)841-5300
www.tnc.org

The Nature Conservancy buys and protects land to save our world's rare plants and animals from extinction. To date, over 12 million acres have been protected, including rain forests, prairies, wetlands, mountains, and beaches.

Reading Is Fundamental
(877)RIF-READ
www.rif.org

Reading Is Fundamental's (RIF) community-based programs give new, free books to America's neediest children so they become lifelong readers and learners. Helps all kids reach their full potential.

Ronald McDonald House Charities
(630)623-7048
www.rmhc.org

The Ronald McDonald House Charities creates, finds, and supports programs that improve the health and well-being of children through its network of 170 local Chapters and 210 Houses in 35 countries.

Salvation Army World Service Office (SAWSO)
(800)638-8079
www.salvationarmy.org

The Salvation Army assists the poor with health services, HIV/AIDS
education, institutional development, income generation, relief, and
reconstruction assistance with a heart to God and hand to humankind.

Santa's Gift
(847)784-8520
www.helzberg.com

The Santa's Gift program began out of Jeff Comment's desire to bring
hope to hospitalized children during the holidays. A visit from Santa
delivering an "I Am Loved"® teddy bear to hospitalized or disadvantaged children is the foundation of this program. For information on
how to start a workplace program, including details on Santa's
Workshop training sessions, visit the Web site.

Shriners Hospitals for Children
(800)241-4438
www.shrinershq.org

These hospitals provide free orthopedic and burn-injury care to children in need. Since opening in 1922, more than a half-million children have been helped.

USA Freedom Corps
(877)USA-Corps
www.usafreedomcorps.gov

Launched during President Bush's 2001 State of the Union address, the USA Freedom Corps is working to encourage all Americans to respond to President George Bush's call to service and to offer them expanded service opportunities through community-based organizations like the Citizen Corps, the AmeriCorps, Senior Corps, and Learn and Serve America programs at the Corporation for National and Community Service, and the Peace Corps.

United Way of America
(703)836-7100
www.unitedway.org

As the nation's leading community solutions provider, United Way invests in and activates the resources to make the greatest possible impact in communities across America. The United Way movement includes approximately 1,400 community-based United Way organizations. Each is independent, separately incorporated, and governed by local volunteers.

World Vision
(888)511-6592
www.worldvision.org

World Vision is an international organization of Christians in nearly 100 countries responding to the physical and spiritual needs of the poor by tackling the root causes of poverty. Our goal is to help families, and children in particular, to realize their full, God-given potential.

World Wildlife Fund
(202)293-4800
www.worldwildlife.org

The Wildlife Fund protects endangered wildlife and their threatened habitats by providing emergency assistance and long-term support to parks, nature reserves, and antipoaching activities on five continents.

YouthBuild USA
(617)623-9900
www.youthbuild.org

Through the support of this organization, unemployed young adults acquire construction skills, complete their high school education, and receive leadership training while constructing or renovating homes for low-income and homeless people.

- 12.5 million: Number of acres in the United States protected by The Nature Conservancy. *Source:* The Nature Conservancy
- 120,000: Number of homes built worldwide by Habitat for Humanity. *Source:* Habitat for Humanity
- 200 million: Number of books distributed nationwide since 1966 by Reading Is Fundamental. *Source:* Reading Is Fundamental